Acclaim for
The Courage of a Samurai

If you only read one book about personal development, this is it! The message is timeless, and the timing is perfect. Lori's book is content-rich bursting with ideas, principles, and stories that will inspire and move you forward in your life. What *kaizen* (philosophy of continuous improvement) was in the 80s, this book is for today. As a Japanese American, this book reinforces the best values and principles of my heritage.

—Daniel C. Russ, Esq.
JAG (Military Lawyer) and Private Practice
Lt Colonel, Staff Judge Advocate, USAF, (Retired)

During the post-WWII occupation of Japan, my father served in the Military Intelligence Service (MIS) where he met and married my mother. Thus, my roots—and identity—are planted in the two worlds of America and Japan. Lori Tsugawa Whaley's book, *The Courage of a Samurai,* is both an insightful exploration of the legacy of the samurai and a heartfelt personal journey of discovery about the samurai's lasting influence on Japanese culture, values, and way of life.

–Clarence Moriwaki, President, Bainbridge Island
Japanese American Exclusion Memorial Association

Say what you mean, mean what you say, and then do it. Making a commitment to make a difference in the world calls for staking a claim about what you believe and living an honest, meaningful life to bring that dream to fruition. This book will change lives and provides a call-to-action for the reader to look inside and reflect on their own personal strengths that hopefully includes a strong sense of integrity. Bravo! This book will be a must-read for men and women globally!

—Linda Ellis Eastman, CEO The Professional Woman Network (PWN)

The samurai class officially ended with the Meiji Reformation in the late 19th century. Yet, the spirit of the samurai is so deeply ingrained into the Japanese character and culture to such an extent that an understanding of *bushido* is a key to understanding modern Japan. Lori's book, *The Courage of a Samurai,* provides valuable insights into the people and culture of this very special country.

—George Yen, DTM International President 2013-2014 Toastmasters International

I was born and raised in Japan so I am fortunate to grow up with the bushido code as part of my culture. After moving to North America, and training in traditional Karate for over 25 years, I realize even more how significant the bushido code is in my daily life. I am so grateful for Lori to open up and share the code with the western world. This book tells you how it feels to live a balanced and fulfilling life!

—Akiko Yoshii-Johnson, Karate-ka, Personal Trainer, Wellness & Lifestyle Coach

In this book you will be introduced to Mr. Chiune Sugihara, otherwise known as the *Japanese Schindler*. Your life will not be the same as you read about the courage and compassion of an unsung hero saving thousands of Jewish lives during World War II. This book is a must add to your personal library as it will inspire you and your family for generations to come.

—Patrick Snow, International Best-Selling Author,
Creating Your Own Destiny* and *Boy Entrepreneur

The Courage of a Samurai inspires you to develop the mindset of a winner in your personal and business life. Using the seven ancient wisdom principles, the author guides you effortlessly in discovering your ultimate excellence and true courage, and she leads you on a path to business and personal fulfillment.

—Susan Friedmann, CSP International Best-Selling
Author, *Riches in Niches: How to Make
it BIG in a Small Market*

The samurai never backed down, never made excuses, and their unwavering courage was remarkable. They possessed something other warriors didn't: bravery of spirit. This book is fascinating and a must read.

—Arvee Robinson, International Speaker and Author

The Courage of a Samurai is an amazing book chock full of useful strategies for small business owners and leaders. I love the chapter on integrity; that is one of the most important characteristics of a successful leader. Lori Tsugawa Whaley illustrates how the samurai bushido code can be applied to everyday life. The book is comprehensive and includes other real world examples. She even shares the biblical story of Joseph as a model of integrity. You'll marvel at the heroic stories of the samurai and be motivated by the sacrifices they made in the name of honor. Grab a copy and read it today!

—Rick Cooper, President, Social Media Outcomes

You will be immediately drawn to the author's view and experience as a Japanese American baby boomer searching for knowledge in the form of tradition and culture from her ancestral hearth. We learn that exemplars of the ancient samurai remain with us today and that we would be best served to remember and honor the best of our past as we move forward in time.

—A. Daktari Alexander, Ph.D.
Executive Director, Interaction Transition

Bushido, samurai code of ethics, prepares each of us to see what is important in life. It is truly the foundation for being a great human being.

—Patsy Surh O'Connell, Founder/President
Asia Pacific Cultural Center

Ms. Whaley writes an incredibly inspirational and impeccably wise read. I just know that this book will continue to garner greater and greater exposure and praise!

—Chris Brusatte, Exhibit Manager
Go For Broke National Education Center

THE COURAGE OF A
SAMURAI

Lori Tsugawa Whaley

THE COURAGE OF A
SAMURAI

Seven Sword-Sharp Principles for Success

LORI TSUGAWA WHALEY

AVIVA
PUBLISHING
New York

Published by:
Aviva Publishing
Lake Placid, NY
www.AvivaPubs.com

Address all inquiries to:
Lori Tsugawa Whaley
Email: Lori@LoriWhaley.com
www.LoriWhaley.com

Third Edition

Editor: Mike Jenkins
Cover & Interior Design: Fusion Creative Works, www.fusioncw.com

ISBN: 978-1-938686-82-5
Library of Congress # 2014922060

6 8 10 12 14 16

Dedicated to my paternal Grandparents Masaichiro and Kazuno Ishii Tsugawa from Tokushima, Japan, and to my maternal Grandparents Kenkichi and Jun Nishiguchi Taniguchi from Matsusaka, Japan. In the early 1900s, all of you braved the Pacific Ocean to settle in a new land in search for a better life, and you gifted me with a rich heritage.

To my parents, George and Mable Tsugawa, who taught me by example the bushido code and to do my best, try my hardest, and never give up…*ganbaru*! Although I did not appreciate working hard on the farm and growing up in the country until later in life, this shaped my character. Thank you for all of life's lessons that you instilled in me.

To my Traumatic Brain Injury (TBI) team, especially the late Vern S. Cherewatenko, MD, MEd, who instilled hope, expert advice and was with me on this entire journey. Thank you from the bottom of my heart. I would also like to acknowledge Dr. Robert

Ahn, DC, CMUA, Channa Beckman, M.A., CCC-SLP, Christy Campbell, LMP, Teri Dodson, CCC/SLP, Theodore S. Kadet, OD, Dr. Tess Mandapat, Dr. Richard E. Seroussi, and Craig E. Taft, PT, MOMT. With utmost gratitude, I would like to thank Leonard Semenea, DC, JD, who demonstrated through his character and action the integrity and compassion of a samurai. Without all of you, your expertise and dedication, this book would not have been possible, and for that I am forever thankful.

To He'Ari Seattle Israeli Dancing for providing excellent instruction and a space to learn and grow. A special thank you to Ellie Morhaime and Dianne Casper for being outstanding instructors and faithful leaders. Dancing was instrumental in my TBI recovery physically and mentally and I always look forward to the dance sessions.

To the God of Abraham, Isaac, and Jacob. Thank You for giving me life and showering me with Your love, mercy and grace.

To the samurai of pre-industrial Japan: I am thankful for your lives of courage, honor, and integrity. Also to the modern-day and future samurais who apply the samurai principles to their lives, lead by example, and make this world a better place.

To you, the reader: may you be inspired by the samurai to do the right thing in all your endeavors. Do your best, try your hardest, never give up, go for broke. . .*ganbatte!*

Literature is the art of discovering something extraordinary about ordinary people, and saying with ordinary words something extraordinary.

—Boris Pasternak

The Tsugawa family *kamon* (crest) is a
combination of the *katabami* plant (wood sorrel)
and three stylized *ken* (swords). The katabami
symbolized a strong family bloodline, and is
one of the five main crests of Feudal Japan. The
sword is symbolic of the warrior and would only
be used by samurai families. Thus the
design is ken katabami.

Contents

Foreword

Lori Tsugawa Whaley hones in on the most significant and memorable aspects of the samurai warrior that we all can imagine within ourselves and others. You will be immediately drawn to the author's view and experience as a Japanese American baby boomer searching for knowledge in the form of tradition and culture from her ancestral hearth. Through Whaley, we see that the samurai warrior is a master, teacher, and philosopher, and we begin to understand why the spirit and the meaning of the samurai transcend. We learn that exemplars of the ancient samurai remain with us today and that we would be best served to remember and honor the best of our past as we move forward in time.

Whaley takes us through a special journey intertwined with admiration, pride, grief, struggle, sadness, respect, and hope. In a most thoughtful way, we understand the samurai warrior as most humane, and because of this, we become more conscious, engaged and more present in the world.

—A. Daktari Alexander, Ph.D.
Executive Director, Interaction Transition

Acknowledgments

First and foremost, I would like to acknowledge and thank John Whaley, my faithful husband of nearly 40 years. You have spent countless hours reading the manuscript, giving advice, and standing beside me in the process of writing this book. Because of you, this book is now a reality.

Domo arigato gozaimasu (thank you in Japanese) to my editor, Mike Jenkins. Living and working in Japan has given you expert insight and understanding of Japan and the Japanese culture. Your advice, knowledge, sense of humor, and encouragement have been invaluable, and for that I am grateful. You have a Japanese heart.

Speaking of encouragement, I would like to thank my book coach, Patrick Snow, for your knowledge and positive attitude that always propelled me forward.

Also, a special thanks to Chris Brusatte, Go For Broke National Education Center, whose enthusiasm, energy, and unwavering support bolstered my spirit in this endeavor.

A sincere acknowledgment and heartfelt thank you to all of you who contributed your time, talent, gifts, expertise and advice: Anne Akabori, Jim Alan, Kim Chaney, Edale Clark, Ron Magden, Ph.D., Karen Matsumoto, Denise Moriguchi, Phil Tajitsu Nash, and Belinda Timpke.

Thank you to Shiloh Schroder and the Fusion Creative Works team for designing the book cover and typesetting. Your guidance, excellent service and expertise were vital for the completion of this book.

A heartfelt acknowledgment to my mentors, both past and present: Sara Little Turnbull, Klemmer & Associates, Empowermax, Arvee Robinson, Eric Lofholm, Rick Cooper, Pastor Mark Biltz, Darnyelle A. Jervey, and Star Bobatoon, Esq.

A special thank you and acknowledgment to my sisters, Mary Lynn Archer and Karen Tsugawa. You encouraged me and looked forward to the completion of this book with great anticipation. Mother was right...we would all be great friends!

Preface

I was born shortly after World War II in a primarily rural Caucasian community disconnected from my Japanese heritage. In fact, I did not realize that I was different until my grade school classmates teased me about it; this was my first encounter with prejudice. I was blamed for the bombing of Pearl Harbor and World War II—a heavy burden on young shoulders, but there was something inside that would not allow the pain I felt to defeat me.

After graduating from college in 1978 with a Bachelor of Arts Degree, I had the fortunate opportunity to work at the Tacoma Art Museum in Tacoma, Washington. I was the assistant to the curator, international designer Sara Little Turnbull, who became my first mentor. At only four feet 11 inches, she has been described as a *giant in design* and *the mother of invention*. Sara had spent time researching in Japan and loved Japanese culture, so she encouraged me to explore my Japanese heritage. My assignment was to research and catalog the artifacts in the "Sara Little Center for Design Research," many of which came from Japan. I became fascinated with the beauty, ingenuity, and simplicity of the Japanese artifacts, and the research consumed me. She always said that I was more Japanese than I realized and suggested that I travel to Japan. Sara referred to herself as my *Jewish mother*. It was God's plan for me to connect with and appreciate my Japanese heritage.

In 1994, I attended an exhibit at the Wing Luke Museum in Seattle, Washington, featuring Chiune Sugihara, also known as the Japanese Schindler. The exhibit described Sugihara's work in saving the lives of the Jewish refugees in Lithuania just before World War II. His courage deeply moved me and another seed was planted regarding my Japanese heritage.

Later in 2003, I watched the movie, *The Last Samurai,* and I felt a connection to the emotional strength of the Japanese characters. My study on the subject of the samurai and the bushido code commenced. These two events caused me to turn pain into gain and embrace that which I once scorned. They also served as the impetus for this book. I am a *sansei* (third-generation Japanese American) and a descendant of the samurai warrior on the paternal side of my family.

Since my initial trip to Japan in 1982, I have returned numerous times to study, visit, and have a deeper connection to my Japanese heritage. I have been reading, writing, interviewing, and studying relentlessly to search for answers; this is my passion and purpose in life. This book represents a step of discovery and my journey home.

This search also has given me the opportunity to understand the qualities of leadership. Although these are not principles unique to Japan, this study has helped me to embrace my Japanese heritage with pride. It has also opened my eyes to how far from these principles we as a society have moved.

Not long ago, there was a time when your word was your bond, and it was safe to leave your doors unlocked because you knew your neighbors. In our modern society, it would seem that the distinction between right and wrong gave way to situational ethics. The term *honest business dealing* is almost considered an oxymoron. Have we succumbed to mediocrity? Are there leaders today worth following?

Are you concerned about the direction our society seems to be taking? Do you feel concern not only for yourself, but also for younger generations such as your children, grandchildren, and great grandchildren? Is it your desire to leave this earth a better place because of you and your contributions?

Life is full of challenges. Tests and trials can allow a stronger you to emerge. In order to survive and grow in these difficult times, do you know how to weather the storm? Do you have a strategy in place to overcome the challenges that you face?

This determination to survive challenges was ingrained in the Japanese immigrants who settled in America through the bushido code. This feudal code provided moral and ethical structure that allowed them to survive and prosper in a country often hostile to their very presence. The *issei* (first-generation Japanese immigrants to the United States) taught the bushido code of honor, loyalty to family and country, and to always do one's best to their children. The *niseis* (second-generation Japanese Americans) were the generation who weathered life behind barbed wire during World War II. They also volunteered to serve their country in both Europe and Asia.

Throughout this book, you will learn the principles of the samurai and be inspired by how these principles influenced their descendants. You will also discover why these principles became the basis for great leadership. Bushido literally means the way of the warrior; it is the code of chivalry developed by the warriors of ancient Japan known as the samurai. This code formed the basis of their conduct. It emphasized courage, loyalty, and the idea of death before dishonor. Over the centuries, it influenced not only the samurai warriors, but also all of Japanese society.

The bushido code includes the following principles:

- Courage
- Integrity
- Benevolence
- Respect
- Honesty
- Honor
- Loyalty

The samurai, or warrior class, evolved from powerful clans banded together as a means of resistance to the encroachment of imperial power. Their principles embraced a sense of order, honor, selflessness, and moral integrity. They understood those imbued with power were required to wield it for the good of the many, not for the selfishness of the few. The samurai dedicated his life to uphold these principles, and such dedication was not optional. He also served and protected his lord, and those in his care. Bushido code principles were not only for the samurai warriors but were a code of ethics that can be utilized and practiced in our everyday life both personally and professionally. In this book, each principle is discussed with examples of people who embody these principles.

At the end of the book, a chapter discusses the Japanese word ganbaru, loosely translated as do your best, try your hardest, never give up, and go for broke! There are several translations for this one word ganbaru because as it so often happens in the Japanese language, there are words describing more of a feeling and state of mind. I believe that ganbaru summarizes the bushido code. Samurai are known to Westerners as having the ability to possess many different characteristics of the bushido code. These may include serving people, striving for honor, and doing one's best.

A colleague and author, Bruce Brummond, wrote a befitting and timeless acronym for the word samurai below:

- **S**trategically
- **A**ctivating
- **M**ilitary
- **U**nderpinnings
- **R**esults in
- **A**bsolute
- **I**ntegrity

I wrote this book to bring honor to the courageous men and women who dedicated their lives by adhering to the bushido code whether they knew it or not. They determined to do the right thing all the time. Their decisions sometimes cost them dearly, but our lives are forever enriched because of their sacrifices.

My goal is to inspire, educate, and empower you, the reader, to take action in your personal and business lives. I believe that you were born to live a life of courage, honor, and integrity, and I would love to be your coach, mentor, and accountability partner on this journey. If you are just beginning, welcome! If you are well on your way, I hope you will be inspired to continue and achieve your highest goals, dreams, and visions. Regardless of where you are, let us link arms, and travel this journey together! You can live a life of honor in today's society. Let the principles of the ancient samurai code guide you along that path.

Are you ready to embark on an incredible journey? Are you open to an honorable way of living in your personal and business lives? Do you want to learn what the ancient principles of the samurai teach about overcoming your challenges? If you are ready, then sharpen your sword, and let's begin!

A year from now, you will wish you started today.
—Karen Lamb

Lori

Lori Tsugawa Whaley

BUSHIDO NO OKITE

Japanese Kanji
for
The Code of Bushido

Introduction

The samurai and their chivalrous code of conduct known as bushido influenced the whole of Japanese society, but who were the samurai and how could a class of people dedicated to war and violence have such an impact on a culture known for its politeness, manners, and aesthetic beauty?

The word samurai literally means "one who serves," and originally referred to domestic servants. Over time, it became attached to those elite military warriors from the nobility who provided security and a fighting force for the aristocratic class. The first samurai could be considered imperial mercenaries.

As imperial family members left the capital in an effort to serve the family name and open new territory outside the capital, the need for more such warriors increased. In conjunction with the expansion of imperial aristocratic needs, a growing segment of nonaristocrats—wealthy landowners—began to create private armies to protect and expand their own holdings.

Though primarily from noble families, the samurai were not considered part of the aristocracy. Instead, they served as the mercenary tools of the various competing groups within the aristocracy. However, their military success for the various aristocratic families resulted in grants of considerable parcels of land to these aristocratic families. In turn, this land came under the administration of their samurai vassals. Eventually the land came under samurai control as payment for their services. Since possession of land was the basis of power, the samurais' power inevitably grew also.

Power struggles and battles between various factions using samurai armies throughout the country persisted for decades. By the late 12th century, the samurai's power had become dominant. As a result, the emperor established the first *shogun* or military dictator. This appointment established a pattern whereby samurai would rule Japan for most of the next seven centuries. The establishment of martial rule and ascension of samurai as the dominant class would have far-reaching effects on the development of Japanese society. Samurai political dominance exerted influence not only in the areas of ruler and lawgivers, but also as patrons in the fields of education and the arts.

It was during the time of the Tokugawa regime (1603-1867) that samurai influence truly started to permeate all aspects of Japanese society. During this period, Japan became a society closed to the outside world. With the unification of the country under a central military government and the exclusion of western influence, this rigid feudal structure produced a nation possessing an unbelievably disciplined nature that is in some respects still evident in Japan today.

From a ruling class birthed in conflict, a concern grew that the material prosperity of the Tokugawa Era would lead to a weakening of the warrior spirit. This was viewed as a threat to the moral and social order of society. Out of this concern, a codification of the traditional practical philosophies of the samurai became a foundational norm for Japanese society at large.

Bushido, or the "way of the warrior," became a guide in moral and practical instruction: a Japanese code of chivalry outlining the personal, social, and professional standards of conduct for the samurai.

The feudal and military modes of this code became ingrained in not only the warrior, but in the society. All aspects of life, including personal responsibility, familial relations, public duties, education, finance, and ethics became embraced through the martial spirit of bushido.

There is no greater symbol of the samurai warrior and the martial code he lived by than his sword. The sword was considered the soul of the samurai. What makes this sword unique is its forging process. The finest materials were combined and repeatedly fired, folded, and hammered. The many repetitions of this process produced a blade with a soft, non brittle center core surrounded by a thin layer of hard steel. A blade strong and resilient—perfect for the samurai sword. As a final procedure, the master sword smith applied a layer of special adhesive clay to the blade, leaving only the edge exposed. When polished this pattern provided a unique look and character for the sword.

The samurai sword is a masterpiece of strength, flexibility and beauty: a true representation of the samurai legacy. In many ways this unique weapon symbolizes not only the samurai, but also the Japanese society that resulted. The properties of strength combined with flexibility became witness to the world following the devastating earthquake and tsunami of March 11, 2011. The world saw a people bend, but not break; a people imbued with human toughness, resolve to carry on, and do what needed to be done without complaint or chaos; a people who embraced moral and ethical wisdom, and put it into action. This can be summed up in the expression: *Do the right thing all the time.* Evident even today, this philosophy is ingrained into all aspects of Japanese life and is the samurais' legacy.

The sword can also be seen as a metaphor for life. As the materials are repeatedly heated, hammered, and folded, the dross is removed, and the elemental properties are combined and enhanced in the fiery furnace, creating a stronger and more flexible material.

In life we often encounter our own 'fiery furnace(s)' or challenges. These tend to mold our character, ultimately producing a stronger, wiser, and more flexible you.

The world's people witnessed Japan arising from a war-torn country into an economic superpower, and they were astonished. Many businesses and organizations desired to study and emulate the concepts behind the Japanese business model; for example kaizen, which means constant improvement. In Japanese businesses and organizations, there is more of a team atmosphere than in western society. The Japanese mindset is toward the good of all and more of a group mentality.

After the 2011 earthquake and tsunami, the people of Japan rose to the occasion. They helped and shared with each other in the face of the disaster. This showed the world the strength and goodness of Japanese moral and ethical integrity in the face of tragedy. Their example is an inspiration for our business and personal lives. It lets us see what this "way of the warrior" is all about. Ask yourself, "What would the samurai do?"

Among the pantheon of warriors,
the samurai is surely the greatest.

—Tetsuro Shigematsu
samurai descendant

Chapter One

COURAGE

勇

YUUKI

Japanese Kanji
for
Courage

Yuuki

COURAGE

*One isn't necessarily born with courage,
but one is born with potential. Without
courage, we cannot practice any other
virtue with consistency. We can't be kind,
true, merciful, generous or honest.*

—Dr. Maya Angelou

Webster describes courage as mental or moral strength to venture, persevere, and withstand danger, fear, or difficulty. In Japanese, *yuuki* is the *kanji* for the English word courage. Kanji is the ancient Japanese form of writing originally derived from the Chinese characters or ideograms. These ideograms were used to represent thoughts or objects. The combination of ideograms provided a means to convey more complex concepts, thoughts, ideas or expression. This word yuuki is composed of two characters. The first kanji *yuu* means bravery or heroism. The second kanji *ki* means spirit or mind. Combined they give the Japanese equivalent of the English word courage. Yuuki is literally translated bravery of spirit.

It's what my mom and dad called having *guts*; the ability to act, to take a chance, to engage…because deep inside there is something telling you there is more. There is something that everybody else overlooks: a chance to seize an opportunity or to just plain *do what is right.*

This concept of courage is the ability to confront hardship or danger and act rightly in the face of it. On occasion, this could entail ridicule, loss of relationships, personal and financial distress, imprisonment, and even death. What does it take to carry on with courage in the face of adversity? Why do some people have the tenacity to risk physical, mental, or personal danger to triumph over hardship?

There are different aspects of courage that range from risk of physical harm to mental endurance and resolve. Courage takes both physical and mental stamina to triumph over adversities. Courage is not reckless or negligent. One must take into consideration the dangers and risks involved in acting with courage. The courageous weigh the risks, and then act for the service of a greater cause.

From the beginning of time, stories of courage have inspired mankind. Examples are the biblical story of David, the young shepherd boy who dared to face the giant Goliath who defied the army and the God of Israel; and the Spartan King Leonidas who, with his small band of warriors, faced down the massive Persian army at Thermopylae and fought to the last man.

What is it that made these people different? Most noticeably they were warriors, willing to contend, to strive, and to persevere for something that they believed. These individuals are remembered for their physical courage. Each of us faces situations that challenge what we believe about our business, our dreams, and ourselves. It is this ability to strive and persevere in the face of these challenges that determines our level of courage.

The samurai warriors of Japan were willing to fight and die for their principles. They regarded their sacred duty to their lord more important than their own lives. Upholding the bushido code was their sole purpose in life.

People act courageously to protect lives daily: law enforcement, firefighters, and those serving, past and present, in our armed forces. We owe them much gratitude.

It is not only physical courage that we admire; we also admire mental and spiritual courage. Thomas Edison developed the light bulb after thousands of failures. Helen Keller, who became deaf and blind at a young age, dared to conquer her world of silence and darkness to pave the way for her own and future generations. Walt Disney and Colonel Sanders endured financial hardship, ridicule, and many rejections before realizing their dreams. In more recent times, you may recognize the name of Captain Chesley B. Sullenberger III, who courageously navigated his troubled aircraft to safety over the Hudson River, saving the lives of all on board.

After being defeated in World War II, Japan rapidly directed its attention and energy to create new products and businesses. With samurai spirit and determination, Japan rose to be an economic superpower in a very short period of time. In awe, the rest of the world attempted to duplicate Japan's achievements by studying its business methods.

The miracle that transformed war-ravaged Japan to the present-day economic powerhouse took courage on the part of the government, industry, and people. We saw this same courageous spirit acted out in the face of the tsunami on March 11, 2011. The level of devastation witnessed along the northeastern coast of Japan was heart wrenching. Yet, in spite of the loss of life and property, people summoned the courage and will to rebuild and continue. This samurai spirit inhabits the souls of modern-day Japan as surely as it did in the days of the shogun.

As you are about to read, the Japanese consul to Lithuania prior to World War II, Chiune Sugihara, faced the most difficult decision of his life. Did he obey the governments of Lithuania and Japan, thereby denying exit visas for Jewish people to escape Nazi annihilation? Or did he obey the voice within directing him to do what he knew was right? What would you do in this situation? We are continually confronted with decisions that test our character. How do you summon the courage to make the decision that may take your business in a different direction? To enter unchartered waters that will change your life? It is often expedient doing what is easy, but is it the *right* or *best* thing for you?

As we saw in the Japanese kanji character for courage, there is a melding of bravery and spirit. We understand bravery because we see its manifestation in actions. The concept of spirit is not as easily grasped in terms of our physical world. Spirit, in this sense, is the intent behind the action. We might even say one's intent produces bravery or courage needed to perform the action. If you are struggling in a decision in your business or your personal life, examine the outcome you desire. Is your intent strong enough to muster the courage you need to take action?

Remember, courage is not being foolhardy, but rather a determination to succeed in spite of circumstances. Count the cost, but don't let fear of failure be the determining factor. It is often better to try and fail than not try at all. The samurai was taught to control his fear and use it to motivate him to excel by focusing on the honor of his commitment. Like the samurai, you too can face your battles with courage.

I learned that courage was not the absence of fear,
but the triumph over it.
The brave man is not he who does not feel afraid,
but he who conquers it.

—Nelson Mandela

Chiune Sugihara

Born on a cold and auspicious day—January 1, 1900—Chiune Sugihara was the second son of five boys and one girl born to Yoshimizu and Yatsu Sugihara, a middle-class samurai family.

Chiune Sugihara's samurai heritage would influence his character and life's path.

Sugihara was an outstanding student and a source of pride for his father. He graduated from high school with high honors. His father planned his future, desiring his enrollment in a prestigious medical school in Korea. At this point in history, Korea was occupied as part of Japan. Even though Sugihara disliked the sight of blood and would not choose to be a doctor himself, he tried to follow the mores of his time. Yoshimizu, his father, had the mindset that his son would be a doctor.

An important trait of a Japanese son or daughter is *oya koko,* to show respect for one's parents. Not wanting to disappoint his father, Sugihara refrained from discussing his desire to learn and teach languages. He obediently went to the appointed medical school entrance examination even though he was in turmoil. Did he follow his father's wishes or follow his heart's desire to study foreign languages and travel the world?

In a moment of decision, the best thing
you can do is the right thing to do.

—Theodore Roosevelt

On the medical entrance exam, Sugihara wrote his name on the exam paper but answered none of the questions indicating that he did not take the test. It took tremendous courage for him to defy his father and follow a different path. Up until this time, he was a model son. However, because of his disobedience, his father's obligations to him ended.

Often, the "status quo" simply produces mediocrity. In order to grow, you may have to swim against the stream; this has its own risks. Mavericks may often fail, but that spirit within gives them the courage to rise again. Sugihara was a maverick, dared to be different, and acted upon what he knew was his life's path. How many Japanese boys in that position, particularly at that time, would take such a risk? Today, how many people would be willing to risk everything to do what they know is the right thing? Are you willing to take such a risk?

Sugihara's decision not to follow his father's wishes took tremendous courage, particularly at this time in the Japanese society. The samurai traditions were still evident, especially within the family hierarchy. He understood his mind and the path he was to follow. With true samurai determination, Sugihara followed what he thought was right for him. Through this one act, he risked not only loss of the financial support needed to further his education, but also the emotional support of his father and the culture at large. Few of us face such a potential life-altering decision at this young age. Would we have the courage to challenge the status quo, to *risk it all*, to do what we know to be right in our heart? This went against everything he learned in childhood, because a good samurai is taught to obey orders.

Now on his own, Sugihara enrolled at Tokyo's prestigious Waseda University in 1918 to study English literature. It was while he studied here that he answered an ad issued by the Japanese foreign ministry seeking recruits. Potentially qualified candidates were encouraged to apply for generous scholarships. There were many requirements and difficult tests to pass; most candidates studied for two to three years. Instead, he had only several months to prepare and execute a plan to advance his education. With samurai determination and intensive studying, he passed this difficult exam and qualified for a scholarship. He displayed intelligence, fortitude, and leadership qualities. Sugihara would later write a manual that covered his method of studying and passing a test focusing on the importance of reading and developing vocabulary; *A Letter from Harbin on a Snowy Day*. His ability to plan would serve him and humanity well by saving thousands of lives at a critical time in history.

Through this scholarship, Sugihara's education continued in Manchuria at Harbin Gakuin where he studied Russian. Harbin Gakuin emphasized service to others, a philosophy that he embraced. He excelled in Russian, and this opened many doors. In 1920, he was drafted into the Japanese army. He spent one year in Korea during his year of mandatory military service.

In 1924, Sugihara returned to Harbin, completed his required courses, and graduated. He was hired by the

Japanese foreign embassy, where he served in the Russian section in Harbin. By 1932, his Russian proficiency made him a rising star within the Japanese governmental services. Shortly thereafter, the Manchurian foreign ministry hired him as an interpreter in the Russian section of the Manchurian foreign office. His next position was Deputy Representative of the same office.

By this time, the Japanese Imperial Army asserted a strong influence on the Manchurian Foreign Ministry and its policies. The sight of military brutality directed toward the Chinese civilian population became unbearable for Sugihara. He was faced with a decision to either further his career, or follow his conscience. Though pressured by superiors, once again he chose to do what he believed was right. His mind made up, Sugihara wrote a letter of protest against Japanese military brutality, and then he resigned his position.

We see in his actions Sugihara's true character. We must remember that he made decisions at a time when Japanese nationalism was on the rise. He understood the risk he was taking regarding not only his career, but also perhaps his own life. In his actions, we see the underlying spirit of bushido on display. We understand in this one individual character trait the reason the samurai were fearsome yet noble individuals.

Sugihara returned to Japan in 1935. The Japanese foreign ministry overlooked his resignation and hired him for Ministry service. During this time period, he met and married Yukiko Kikuchi who would be by his side throughout the coming ordeals.

Chiune and Yukiko Sugihara became the proud parents of their first son, Hiroki, a year after they were married. Shortly after Hiroki's birth, the Sugihara family transferred to Finland, where he was assigned as a translator at the Legation in Helsinki. While stationed in Helsinki, they were delighted when their second son, Chiaki, was born.

After two years of service in Finland, Sugihara was reassigned to open up a Consulate in Kaunas, Lithuania. At that time, there was turmoil and unrest throughout Europe. He was assigned to watch German activities along the Russian borders, and skilled in both Russian and German, he was the ideal person for the position. Their third son, Haruki, was born in Kaunas, Lithuania.

While shopping at a store in Kaunus during the winter of 1939, Sugihara overheard the conversation of a young 11-year old boy, Solly Ganor, who wanted money to see a movie. He gave some money to Solly, who in turn invited Mr. and Mrs. Sugihara to their family Jewish Chanukah celebration. Sugihara and his wife Yukiko attended this celebration, and they were reminded of similar Japanese celebrations showing the closeness of family ties. This simple act of kindness would have an impact on many lives in the future.

Sugihara became friends with young Solly Ganor and his father. Because the Ganors were refugees from Russia, they were able to communicate in Russian with each other.

Solly Ganor and his father received visas from Sugihara to cross Russian borders but were not able to use them because of their Russian citizenship. He and his father were later deported to the Landsberg-Kaufering outer camp of Dachau. In an unusual twist of fate, in 1945, the Japanese American soldiers of the 522nd Field Artillery Battalion at Landsberg-Kaufering liberated Solly Ganor. Ironically, the nisei soldiers of the 522nd's families were behind barbed wire in their own country at the same time.

As Hitler tightened his reins around Eastern Europe, time was running out for Jewish peoples' safety. By late July of 1940, hundreds of Jewish refugees came from Poland to Lithuania, desperately trying to escape Nazi persecution. The refugees found their way to the Japanese Consulate because they heard of the possibility of escaping annihilation by obtaining a Japanese visa. Every day, frightened men, women and children pleaded desperately for their lives outside the Japanese Consulate office.

Sugihara was faced with the most difficult decision in his life. Japanese tradition bound him to obedience, but he was a samurai taught to help those in need. He asked permission from the Japanese government three times to assist, but each time he was denied. If he disobeyed his government, he faced disgrace and dishonor. For him to disobey the government was an enormous undertaking that went completely against Japanese tradition. Also, to disobey would cause extreme financial hardship for his family, as well as risking their lives during a difficult time in history.

Sugihara collaborated with others to ensure a successful exit for the Jewish refugees. Dutch Interim Consul Zwartendijk was critical in creating a final destination, the Dutch colony of Curacao and Dutch Guiana, both of which did not require formal entry visas. Without the end destination, the visas would not have been valid. They intentionally left out the Dutch governor's signature.

In order to reach their final destination, the refugees needed to pass through the Soviet Union. The Soviet consul agreed to let them pass if they could obtain a transit visa from the Japanese allowing passage via Japan to their final destination. The plan took much thought and planning, similar to passing the scholarship exam for Harbin Gakuin in Manchuria. The time to execute the plan was short, and they needed to act swiftly.

Sugihara and Yukiko feared for their entire family. Making the decision to help would forever affect their lives; they could face a bleak future or government punishment. Both agreed they did not have a choice. He said at that time,

I may have disobeyed my government,
but if I didn't, I would be
disobeying God.

Sugihara embraced yuuki, literally *bravery of spirit* as his samurai ancestors had done. In the face of danger, he chose to stand for what he knew to be right regardless of the personal cost. He stood on the same foundational beliefs that guided the ancient samurai warriors of long ago.

In occupied Europe, thousands of Jews were being imprisoned and murdered each day. Because of the situation, Sugihara began to write visas on his own initiative in violation of his direct orders. From July

31 to September 4, 1940, he tirelessly handwrote visas for 18 to 20 hours per day. He produced a normal month's worth of visas each day: 200-300 visas. Rarely stopping to eat or rest, he worked on the visas alone, not wanting to jeopardize his family. He did not allow Yukiko to get involved with the visas because he did not want her to be implicated.

Even a hunter cannot kill a bird that
comes to him for refuge.

—Japanese Proverb

During the time Sugihara wrote the transit visas, the Soviet government insisted that he leave Kaunas, and the Japanese Foreign Ministry sent orders to close and vacate the embassy. He ignored both orders and continued to write visas in order to save the lives of Jewish refugees. The Japanese Foreign Ministry finally sent an urgent telegram demanding that he close the consulate, and then depart for Berlin. With sad hearts, the Sugiharas realized it was time to leave.

As the train departed, Sugihara leaned out the window and threw out visas that contained only his signature and the consulate seal to the many left behind. It grieved the

Sugiharas to leave people behind, because their fate was probably death with no way to escape.

Forty-five years after the Soviet invasion of Lithuania, Sugihara was asked his reasons for issuing visas to the Jews. He explained that the refugees were human beings, and that they simply needed help:

You want to know about my motivation, don't you? Well. It is the kind of sentiments anyone would have when he actually sees refugees face to face, begging with tears in their eyes. He just cannot help but sympathize with them. Among the refugees were the elderly and women. They were so desperate that they went so far as to kiss my shoes, Yes, I actually witnessed such scenes with my own eyes. Also, I felt at that time, that the Japanese government did not have any uniform opinion in Tokyo. Some Japanese military leaders were just scared because of the pressure from the Nazis; while other officials in the Home Ministry were simply ambivalent. People in Tokyo were not united. I felt it silly to deal with them. So, I made up my

mind not to wait for their reply. I knew
that somebody would surely complain
about me in the future. But, I myself
thought this would be the right thing to
do. There is nothing wrong in saving many
people's lives.... The spirit of humanity,
philanthropy...neighborly friendship...with
this spirit, I ventured to do what I did,
confronting this most difficult situation---
and because of this reason, I went ahead
with redoubled courage.[1]

After departing Lithuania, the Sugiharas travelled
to Berlin, then Czechoslovakia, Konigsberg, and finally Bucharest, Romania. They stayed in Bucharest until
the end of World War II in 1945. Captured by Russian
soldiers, the family was then incarcerated as prisoners
of war in a Romanian prison camp for approximately
18 months.

During the cold, harsh winter of 1946, the
Sugiharas were released and returned to Japan. Sadly,
their youngest child, Haruki, died shortly after they
arrived. It took approximately one year to return to

---

1. Wikipedia Online, "Chiune Sugihara" http://en.wikipedia.org/wiki/Chiune_Sugihara

Japan because of hardships, delays, and uncertainties of escaping Russia.

After returning to Japan, Sugihara hoped his career would continue. However, he was both humiliated and disappointed when asked by the Ministry to resign. The Japanese Ministry said they were downsizing because of the war. However, because of a private conversation, he surmised the action was related to the incident in Lithuania. In the Japanese culture, "*saving face*" is ingrained, and he grieved the humiliation extended toward his family, but always believed that he had done the right thing.

To support his family, Sugihara worked various jobs as a language tutor, manager for the U.S. government-run PX, or Base Exchange store, and also as a door-to-door salesman. The family suffered hardships and lived in poverty until the early 1960s. He endeavored to persevere despite emotional and financial hardship and lack of recognition. He wanted to do what was right and adhere to the samurai bushido code.

In the mid 1960s, Sugihara found employment as a branch manager for a Japanese trading company in Russia. The job required him to live in Moscow. For sixteen years he was separated from his family a majority of the time. He was able to visit the family twice per year, and he sent the greater part of his wages to Yukiko and his family. He endured hardship, suffering, and lack of recognition to save those he loved knowing he "*did the right thing.*"

In 1968, during one of his visits to Japan, Sugihara received an unexpected call from the Israeli Embassy. Mr. Nishri, an attaché for the Israeli Embassy, was visiting Japan and desired to meet Sugihara at the embassy. Mr. Nishri was a Jewish representative who sought exit visas in Lithuania prior to World War II. He showed Sugihara the visa that he had issued 28 years earlier. Mr. Nishri had been searching for Sugihara for many years to thank him for saving his life. Although Mr. Nishri inquired earlier if others had been saved by the visas, the Japanese government said they had no information. It was an emotional reunion for both men and Sugihara realized that his efforts were not in vain. He later rejoiced when he learned that most of the recipients of the visas had survived!

It is recorded that Sugihara wrote over 2,000 visas during the summer of 1940, resulting in saving over 6,000 lives. Among the survivors was the entire Mirrer Yeshiva, a Jewish institute for religious studies, comprised of over 300 students and staff. Mirrer Yeshiva was the only yeshiva whose entire membership survived the Holocaust. In March 2015, a celebration to honor this achievement took place in Brooklyn, New York. Mr. Nobuki Sugihara, son of Chiune Sugihara, attended the commemorative event. Today it is estimated there are over 100,000 descendants of these survivors who owe their lives to Chiune Sugihara and his family.

If you save the life of one person,
it is as if you saved the world entire.

—Jewish Talmud

In 1985, Chiune Sugihara was recognized as one of the *Righteous Among the Nations* by Yad Vashem, the Holocaust Martyrs and Heroes Remembrance Authority in Jerusalem, Israel. He became the first Asian to receive this award. His wife, Yukiko, and his son, Hiroki, accepted the honor on his behalf because he was not strong enough to travel. In Jerusalem, trees were planted in Sugihara's name, and a park was named in his honor.

Eventually, Sugihara was honored for his contributions and heroism in his own country. At his birthplace in Yaotsu, Japan (Gifu Prefecture), a monument and a museum documenting his courageous efforts were built in his honor. Completed in 1992, this project was financed and supported by the people of Gifu and others, and was appropriately named the *Hill of Humanity*.

During a trip to Japan in October 2010, my husband and I visited the Hill of Humanity in Yaotsu, Japan. It was a deeply moving experience that still continues to affect me. On display were pictures, visas, and mementos that told Chiune Sugihara's story of how he saved so many Jewish refugees; he was a truly courageous samurai. As I walked among the many artifacts, I realized that principles do matter and these can change individuals, businesses, and societies for the better far beyond a lifetime. He counted the cost: he knew in his heart what he had to do, and because of what he believed to be true, he had the courage to act.

At times, you may think *I'm only one person* and feel that you or your contribution is insignificant. However, we see that because of Sugihara's courageous act, thousands of lives were spared and many are affected even today. We all have a calling in our lives, and everyone's gift to humanity is important. It is not your job to compare, but be faithful in what you are given.

If you were offered all of the riches in the world under one condition, would you take it? What if the condition would be for you to give up your sight, smell, touch, thought, speech, hearing, and your taste? Would you still take it? How would you survive and function in this world? What would your life be like? In asking this question to my audiences, there has not been one person who would make the trade. You are so valuable; in fact, you are *priceless!* When you realize your worth, the world around you looks different, and you see people in a new light.

I first learned of Chiune Sugihara at the Wing Luke Museum in 1994 in Seattle, Washington, and his story left a profound impression on me. His life and acts of courage inspired me to write this book and visit Yaotsu, Japan in October, 2010. I am thankful that we visited the memorial museum and Hill of Humanity, because I now have a fuller understanding and greater appreciation of Chiune Sugihara and his worldly impact.

Most importantly, Sugihara was a samurai warrior, yet he did not handle a gun or sword. He brought about change without going to battle. He was strategic, yet peaceful; decisive yet compassionate; and determined yet gentle. He was a peaceful warrior, and not every warrior has to be a battlefield-hardened soldier to be a true warrior and a hero. There are many positive attributes in Chiune Sugihara's life that you can emulate. Which one(s) would you choose?

Sugihara understood his purpose in life at an early age, lived accordingly, and pursued opportunities in alignment with his purpose and values. He did not take the medical school entrance exam, because he knew that was not his purpose in life. He resigned from assignments that he disagreed with because of people's mistreatment. He counted the costs knowing that his decision could mean his death, but as stated earlier, he felt it was most important to obey God. Are you willing to count the cost to fulfill your life purpose?

From Chiune Sugihara's story, you learned about doing the right thing and acting upon your principles. It took more than physical courage for Sugihara to write the visas knowing his life was in jeopardy. This act also took emotional and spiritual courage. By acting upon your principles, you lay a foundation for a solid life with vital relationships. If I asked you if you had a code of honor that you lived by, could you name the elements of your honor code?

As stated earlier, courage takes many forms. Sugihara lived a life of courage. Unlike most, he knew what was right and had the courage to act on his convictions. As we see from his story, courage is not always easy, but it has its own rewards. Chiune Sugihara died knowing that in the face of great danger, he did the right thing!

*And most important, have the
courage to follow your intuition.*

—Steve Jobs

Chapter Two

INTEGRITY

義

GI

Japanese Kanji
for
Integrity

Gi

INTEGRITY

*Integrity is always number one. Put all
of the other character traits in any order you want,
but they all come after integrity.*

—Chris Widener

Webster defines integrity as the quality or state of being of sound moral principle: uprightness, honesty, and sincerity. People associate integrity with values above reproach and the quality of being correct in judgment or procedure. The Japanese translation for *gi* is justice and moral righteousness.

Inherent in the heart of man is a sense of morality: right and wrong. Integrity is doing the right thing because it is both just and proper. Doing the right thing keeps one on the straight and narrow, or on the path of moral righteousness. For the samurai, there were no deviations or bends in the road. When you add integrity to courage, you have an indomitable force for good!

The samurai did not compromise concerning doing what was right—no matter the cost, even to forfeiting one's life. Integrity is the moral compass the samurai used to navigate the narrow path traveled. It is considered so important, that stories illustrating the concept of death before dishonor became popularized worldwide. Perhaps the most familiar to Westerners recounts the true story of how a band of leaderless samurai retainers honored their commitment and avenged the senseless death of their lord. Having achieved their objective, these warriors willingly gave up their own lives as the cost of fulfilling their commitment. These are the famous 47 *ronin*, and they are honored as an example of integrity and the samurai ideals. Even today, they are considered cultural heroes in Japan.

Every moment of each day, you are faced with choices. The ability to choose has its consequences. By choosing integrity's narrow path, you are creating good for all. Your choices touch your life, others' lives, and the lives of future generations. The samurai acted on moral correctness, knowing his decisions affected himself, his family, society, and the future of his lord and country.

The emphasis on one's integrity came to America with the first Japanese immigrants, the issei. This was an important part of the bushido principles that provided the moral and ethical bulwark that allowed them to survive in an often-hostile environment. These principles were passed on to their offspring, the nisei, as a way of defining their Japanese heritage. These principles served the nisei well as they fought the prejudice of the World War II era.

These wounds were still fresh when my generation, the sansei, were born. Subtly, these principles of bushido became a way for us to regain the trust and respect of a nation. Our parents emphasized that our behavior extended beyond ourselves. We represented our own family, the Tsugawa clan, and even the Japanese American community. This was deeply ingrained in me and I seriously took it to heart. In the time period shortly after World War II, people were watching us. Suspicion, animosity, and prejudice were still evident, and we had to prove that we were good citizens. The time in the camps during the war was still a fresh part of my parents' memories. Since their integrity was questioned, this brought great shame to honorable people who committed no crimes.

Your character has both a public and private face. It is in times when no one is observing that your true character is displayed. Did you ever get caught with your hand in the cookie jar? That may have moved you from the fear of being caught to the decision to do the honorable deed. As you mature, your conscience is developed, and you do the right thing because it is the right thing to do.

The samurai did the right thing because of his adherence to the bushido code. He detested unjust behavior and dealings that were underhanded. When the precise Shogunate laws were disobeyed, it could lead to severe punishment or even death. A strict adherence to Shogunate rules created peace and harmony in Japanese society; it made it easier for the samurai to carry out his duty and focus on the task at hand.

In the biblical story, Joseph had the ability to interpret dreams, and he was his father Jacob's favorite son. Jealous of Joseph's status, his brothers sold him into slavery in Egypt. His dream–interpretation abilities allowed Joseph to interpret Pharaoh's dreams. He rose in status and was made viceroy. Famine drove Joseph's brothers to Egypt in search for food. Joseph had the power to deny his brothers' request for food, yet he acted in integrity, forgave his brothers, and saved his family. Joseph was tested, and the integrity of his character prevailed because of his faith in God.

Abraham Lincoln signed the Emancipation Proclamation in 1863. He is quoted as saying, "I never, in my life, felt more certain that I was doing right, than I do in signing this paper." Lincoln faced significant opposition regarding this action, yet the conviction of his moral principles led him to do what he knew to be just and right. His doing the right thing turned the tide and forever changed the United States of America.

In this chapter, we will discuss the life of Michi Nishiura Weglyn, who left a very successful career as a fashion designer to research the subject of the Japanese American incarceration during World War II. She knew what had been done was wrong, and so she endeavored to expose this wrong and restore the dignity of her people, regardless of her own personal cost. Her pioneering book to rectify the injustice inflicted upon her and 120,000 people of Japanese descent helped to lead the way for the Redress Movement of the 1980s.

To the samurai, integrity was a measure of trustworthiness and spoke volumes about someone's character. With absolute adherence to your vision, or tenet, you are laser-focused like the samurai warrior. The samurai committed to his profession because his life depended on it. Together with other positive traits of the samurai, such as courage, honesty, and loyalty, you can experience greater accomplishments because you are at peace with yourself. You need not worry about being a chameleon because there is only one you! If your purpose is to leave the world a better place, then make integrity your intention. Intention is more than a wish, it is a commitment: a determination to uphold your principles regardless of the circumstances. It means doing what you know is right even when it's not popular or convenient—even when no one is watching.

It doesn't mean it will be easy. The world looks for someone who rises above the crowd's mediocrity, who honors his commitments and makes no excuses when he falls short. Such people take responsibility for their words and actions because they own them.

Say what you mean, mean what you say, and then do it. As you put your stake in the ground, you are making a commitment and laying claim to what you believe. Just as the samurai did, you can also make a difference.

Do what is right because it is right,
and leave it alone.

—Chiune Sugihara

Michi Nishiura Weglyn

Raised as a farmer's daughter in Brentwood, California, Michi Nishiura Weglyn endured and overcame hardships to devote her life to making atonement for injustice. She was the elder daughter born to Tomojiro and Misao Nishiura on November 29, 1925.

Tomojiro and Misao Nishiura emigrated from Japan and worked as tenant farmers in Brentwood, California. The family leased land to raise fruits and vegetables. Michi's job was to tend to the farm animals, which she treated as her pets.

After the U.S. entered World War II in December 1941, President Franklin D. Roosevelt signed Executive Order 9066 on February 19, 1942. This order uprooted and forcibly removed 120,000 people of Japanese descent living on the United States west coast from their homes to an unknown future. The Nishiura family was among those affected as well as both of my parents and their families.

They eventually arrived at Gila River War Relocation Center in Arizona after riding on a crowded train for several days. The blinds were drawn so that they did not know where they were going. The living quarters were poorly constructed and surrounded by barbed wire fences 12 feet high. Guard towers held watchmen with guns aimed at them. Anyone who tried to escape was shot.

The family was assigned to a room in Block 66, Barrack 12. They shared the Gila River War Relocation Center with over 13,000 other detained Japanese and Japanese Americans. Life was not easy for the Nishiuras, and privacy was a thing of the past. For the next three years, a single room (approximately 500 square feet) would be their home. Michi remembers using an umbrella for protection from the harsh, hot, and windy conditions, and she often awoke in the morning covered with sand.

Michi was a high achiever and an outstanding student who participated in numerous activities. She applied for and won a scholarship to attend the prestigious Mount Holyoke College in Massachusetts. The full scholarship for commendable students was awarded by the National Japanese American Student Relocation Council and headed by the Quakers. She was a biology major, and she was also gifted in drawing. While attending college, she became fascinated with stage productions, and this began her interest in costume design.

In December 1945, Michi contracted tuberculosis and was forced to withdraw from college. She recovered at Glen Gardner Sanitarium in New Jersey, but did not graduate from college. She suffered a lifetime of frail health aggravated in part by the harsh weather conditions at the incarceration camp in Gila River, Arizona.

Michi continued her education at Barnard College and the Fashion Academy in New York City, but during that time, she was again treated for tuberculosis and spent time at Mt. Kipp Sanitarium in upstate New York.

While a student, Michi met her future husband, Walter Matthys Weglyn, who arrived from Holland following the end of World War II. Walter was of German Jewish descent and survived the Holocaust. In 1939, at the age of 12, his parents sent him and his brother to Holland via Kindertransport, where he was sheltered and went into hiding. He was protected and hidden at 12 different locations to save his life. During that time, Walter's parents were at the Theresienstadt concentration camp in what is now the

Czech Republic. Miraculously, the parents survived the ordeal, and the family was reunited in New York after World War II. During the time Walter went into hiding to save his life in Europe, Michi was incarcerated in Arizona.

Walter and Michi married on March 5, 1950. Initially, their parents opposed the interracial marriage. However, she recalled overhearing her mother brag to an issei friend that her son-in-law was more Japanese than a Japanese. That told Michi that Walter was accepted into the family. They enjoyed a devoted, supportive, and loving relationship throughout their life together.

Michi became a recognized costume designer in the 1960s, designing costumes for the Roxy Theatre, Perry Como, Bob Hope, and Ginger Rogers. Even though she enjoyed success and fame, she was an unassuming person with a humble beginning.

The mid to latter 1960s was a time of turmoil in the United States due to the Viet Nam War and civil rights unrest. There was speculation that the U.S. government might place those protesting the war in concentration camps as a means to control the protest.

That is why in 1968, when Michi received an honorary degree from California State Polytechnic University in Pomona, California, she mentioned Attorney General Ramsey Clark's comment regarding the issue of detaining the Viet Nam war protesters. Clark had said on television we never had, we do not now have, and will not ever have a concentration camp. She knew Attorney General Clark's comment was not true and believed the record regarding her people needed to be rectified.

That same year, Michi discovered the book *While Six Million Died*, written by Arthur D. Morse. The author wrote about the indifference and callousness of the American government regarding the eradication of the Jewish people in Europe. Ironically, at the same time Jewish people were annihilated in the Nazi death camps in Europe, Japanese Americans were incarcerated in the United States. Both were unwanted people in their own country. She wondered if the apathy toward the Jewish people could have contributed to the incarceration of Japanese Americans.

> *Do not follow the crowd when it does*
> *what is wrong; and don't allow*
> *popular view to sway you into*
> *offering testimony for any cause*
> *if the effect will be to pervert justice.*

—Exodus 23:2

Not one to be complacent, Michi embarked on a journey that continued for the rest of her life. She resolved an injustice and worked toward removing the guilt and shame of her people, the Japanese Americans. Her curiosity regarding this incident led her to investigate the truth behind the Japanese American incarceration even though over twenty years had lapsed since leaving the incarceration camp in Arizona.

For seven years, Michi diligently researched the primary documents of the Japanese American incarceration. She made countless trips to the National Archives in Washington D.C., New York City Library, and the Franklin D. Roosevelt Library in New York. She would arrive early in the morning, eat a sandwich for lunch, and then continue her research until closing. She was not funded by grants, but personally bore the expense of travel and time during the entire project. She was unwavering in her quest to uncover the truth. She needed to find answers, and in so doing, set the records straight in order to rectify the injustice she knew was committed.

One can only imagine the volumes of documents, files, and papers involved in the research and writing for her book. This laborious work was accomplished without computers!

Being a Holocaust survivor, Walter Weglyn was supportive and sympathetic of his wife's efforts. He encouraged Michi to write the truth even if it was unpopular or unpalatable. He also was an editor and critic of her work, and understood her quest to discover the truth. In the Acknowledgments of her book, Michi expressed appreciation to Walter for his encouragement and contribution; the project might have been abandoned were it not for his support. So affected were they by the trauma of their childhoods, they remained childless throughout their marriage.

Never apologize for being correct,
or for being years ahead of your time.
If you're right and you know it,
speak your mind.
Even if you are a minority or one,
the truth is still the truth.

—Gandhi

As Michi stated, it was one thing to read about documents, but it was another thing to actually read the documents...face to face. For her, it was a poignant experience to uncover the truth, blaze a trail, and obtain justice for over 80,000 Japanese Americans who were still alive at that time. According to Michi:

It would involve a 180 degree turn on my part from designing to detective work to clear in some possible way my own people; my own self of that stain of dishonor and disgrace.

Before World War II, the winds of war were escalating, and the loyalty of the Japanese Americans was in question. The State Department's investigator, Curtis B. Munson, was commissioned to examine and report on the Japanese American loyalty to the United States. The Munson Report included over ten years of research by the FBI and Navy Intelligence. The report's conclusion did not corroborate the military necessity espoused by the U.S. Government for incarceration. No evidence of disloyalty was reported with the Japanese Americans living in the United States in the event of war. The Munson Report was a well-kept secret that Michi discovered through her extensive research. In spite of its findings, in 1942, President Franklin D. Roosevelt signed Executive Order 9066, forcibly removing some 120,000 Japanese Americans (over 70% were U.S. citizens) into American incarceration camps.

In early 1943, to add insult to injury, the Loyalty Questionnaire was submitted to the Japanese Americans detained at the 10 incarceration camps. This included both citizens and non-citizens 17 years of age and older. Many of those incarcerated were non-citizens because they were issei, first generation immigrants, who had been denied citizenship on the basis of their race. Questions 27 and 28 of the questionnaire were particularly confusing and brought feelings of frustration and resentment. They read:

Question #27: Are you willing to serve in the armed forces of the United States on combat duty wherever ordered?

Question #28: Will you swear unqualified allegiance to the United States of America and faithfully defend the United States from any or all attack by foreign or domestic forces, and forswear any form of allegiance or obedience to the Japanese emperor, or any other foreign government, power, or organization?

The majority of the incarcerates answered yes to both questions, but it was disturbing and confusing for the women, both elderly and young, to agree to go to battle. There were others who refused to sign and answer yes because they felt it was unjust to fight for a country that detained them and their families behind barbed wire. This act violated their Constitutional rights as U.S. citizens.

Those who refused to sign were considered disloyal and segregated at the Tule Lake Segregation Center (renamed in 1943) in northern California. They were referred to as the *No No Boys*. These men exercised their constitutional right by refusing to fight in the U.S. Army. Most were ostracized by other Japanese Americans for their actions. Regardless of how the questions were answered, each responder answered the questions based on the integrity of his/her conviction and was willing to live with the consequences. For the *No No Boys*, the price of acting on their convictions was further incarceration in a federal prison. Their integrity was measured by willingness to face the consequences of their convictions: how would you have answered Questions #27 and #28 if you were in their situation?

In the summer of 2009, my cousin, Pam Oja, and I went on a pilgrimage to Tule Lake in northern California where our mothers were incarcerated during World War II. Although they had not responded *No* to questions #27 and #28, they were at Tule Lake during the first part of World War II. My mother was not physically able to attend and it was probably for the best, as she rarely spoke about her experience in the camp.

Tule Lake detained some 18,000 (at its peak) Japanese American citizens and non-citizens. The first year, there was no plumbing for indoor lavatories. Tule Lake had three sets of barbed wire 12 feet high. Tanks patrolled the premises. The incarcerees' only crime was their race, and it brought shame, humiliation, and confusion to those who had broken no law. Like the samurai, they faced their situation with courage and integrity, and emerged stronger.

We were guided through the "prison within the prison" by Jimi Yamaichi, who helped to construct prison housing for the *No No Boys*. It was ironic and almost seemed unreal to tour the prison within the prison reserved for those who answered "No" to the *loyalty* questions. It is interesting to note here that this took place less than 75 years ago.

My thoughts and feelings were mixed: heartbreak, anger, disbelief, dishonor, and sadness. It was difficult to view and hear about the subhuman conditions that my parents unjustly and illegally experienced. They never spoke of the injustices or the shame they must have endured. I often wonder if I would have faced their situation with their same grace.

After much persuasion, my husband and I convinced my parents to attend the Minidoka Pilgrimage in 2008. Dad remarked that the barracks looked more like the Hilton than what he remembered! Below is how he recounted this period in his life:

In February 1942, President Franklin D. Roosevelt issued Executive Order 9066, which stated that the military could remove all people of Japanese descent who lived within 200 miles of the west coast. By April, our family was to be interned at the Portland Expo Center and was given number #15030, which meant we were the fifteen thousand thirtieth family to receive a number. Each of us was allowed one suitcase; our family was allowed one duffle bag. A Caucasian friend drove us to the livestock pavilion.

At this point, Hank (my elder brother) had been drafted into the U.S. Army and was stationed at the Military Intelligence Service (MIS) language school in Minnesota. He served in the MIS overseas. My younger brother, Akira, was inducted into the U.S. Army shortly after we arrived at Minidoka. He served in the MIS stateside.

The summer of 1942 was hot. The pavilion had housed cattle before it was cleared for us. The floors had been hosed down, but, of course, when the water went down, the smell of manure came up. It was bad. The food was bad. Everybody had diarrhea.

We moved out in September. They loaded us on trains. We were in the dark for three days with all the blinds pulled down, so we wouldn't know where we were going. I don't remember what we did when we needed to use the bathroom! Finally, the train stopped, and we looked out at thousands of acres of sagebrush as far as the eyes could see. Army trucks took us to "camp." We were greeted by machine guns pointed toward us in the gun towers; they probably thought the worst of us. It was frightening and gave me a sense of hopelessness. I thought, "This is our fate?"

Living quarters were arranged in a "block" with the mess hall, recreation room, and bathrooms located in the center, surrounded by barracks. Our room was about 20' x 20' with a light bulb and a potbellied stove fueled by coal. We had no running water in our room, and used a 'communal' shower and initially 'outhouses' for our bathroom. No privacy. We were interned at Minidoka near Twin Falls, Idaho.

Over 9,000 people of Japanese descent lived within the confines of Minidoka; we were assigned to Block

30 near other Portland Japanese people. In the camps, they wanted everybody to do something. My job was to cut the bottoms out of tin cans, and I was paid $14.00 per month. The metals were needed for the war effort. I worked with three other 'buddies,' and we managed to have a good time as we performed our duties. After a while, the guards began to trust us and realize that we were peaceful people.

In October, 1943, there was an emergency; Mom was dying. We had one doctor for all the 9,000 people in camp. By the time Mom got to a doctor and was diagnosed with terminal cancer, there was nothing they could do for her. We were given special permission to leave Minidoka and move to Boise so Mom could get the best care available. The Reverend Harold Johnson provided a lovely home for us at 1410 Sherman Street; there are some nice people in this world.

Mom was released from the hospital to spend her last days with family. In Boise, we saw signs that read, "No Japs Allowed" in restaurants and stores; but in the four-block area of East Avenue where we lived, people treated my youngest brother, Jim, like family. He played football and baseball with the neighborhood children. Only one kid said to him, "Don't come around the house, Jim, because my dad won't like it."

After World War II ended, the Japanese and Japanese Americans were released, and many had nowhere to go. Homes, properties, and businesses were confiscated, stolen, or 'lost' because of unpaid taxes. We could not pay taxes because our bank accounts were frozen. We scattered over different areas of the United States, and we were no longer in our ethnic areas. I think it was good that other Americans got to know us and realize that we were good citizens.

Remarkably, Dad harbors no ill feelings regarding his experience, and willingly shares his story with his friends and relatives, the public, and local students.

In spite of their hardship, the issei, and their children, the nisei, made the most of their situation. The Japanese word *gaman,* means to endure the unbearable with dignity and patience. Art, furniture, tools, woodcarvings, paintings, toys, and everyday objects were created with found materials such as wood, shells, paper, and fabric. The Japanese attention to beauty and detail was remarkable, and their indomitable and persevering spirit is evident in their work.

The Art of Gaman was a traveling exhibit that show-cased more than 120 artifacts crafted by Japanese Americans during their incarceration in camps in World War II. Author Delphine Hirasuna organized and curated the exhibit which began in Washington, D.C., on March 2010, at the Smithsonian American Art Museum, Renwick Gallery. In the summer of 2014, the exhibit traveled to the Bellevue Arts Museum in Bellevue, Washington. The exhibit was well received, and attendees marveled at the indomitable spirit of the Japanese Americans displayed in the artifacts.

The definition of integrity embraces the concepts of uprightness, honesty, and having values above re-proach. These words describe the efforts and person-ality of Michi Nishiura Weglyn. Her desire that the truth about the wartime incarceration of innocent Japanese immigrants and Japanese American citizens be brought to light would require no less.

Michi's book, *Years of Infamy*, is supported by photos of children, people, and life in the incarceration camps. She included these heart-rending photos because a picture is worth a thousand words. Photocopies of government documents and newspaper articles clearly validate the message of the book. She worked diligently, and because of her book's integrity, historical events were corrected, and a maligned people was exonerated.

With her research completed, Michi diligently sought a publisher for her book *Years of Infamy: The Untold Story of America's Concentration Camps.* William Morrow and Company finally published the book in 1976. James Michener wrote the introduction and expressed that Michi shared a story about our national history that deserved telling.

Michi's book helped propel the movement for the restitution of civil rights, apology, and monetary compensation that became known as the Redress Movement of the 1980s. The Movement culminated in the passage of the Civil Liberties Act of 1988, which compensated those living Japanese Americans who were detained unjustly during World War II. In the beginning, activist Edison Uno cited her work in his appeal. Other nisei would follow. The Japanese American Citizen League (JACL) also became involved in redress to assist the Japanese Americans.

To set the record straight regarding the wartime experiences of the West Coast Japanese population, the JACL published a brochure correcting common euphemisms used to explain the action of the U.S. government. The table below lists the common euphemisms on the left with a more accurate description on the right.

SUMMARY TABLE OF ACCURATE TERMS

The table below, constructed from Ishizuka's list (Ishizuka, 2006, p. 72, *Lost and Found: Reclaiming the Japanese American Incarceration*. Urbana & Chicago, IL: University of Illinois Press), summarizes the various euphemistic terms and their more accurate counterparts:

EUPHEMISM	ACCURATE TERM
Evacuation	Exclusion, or forced removal
Relocation	Incarceration in camps; also used after release from camp.
Non-aliens	U.S. citizens of Japanese ancestry.
Civilian exclusion orders	Detention orders.
Any or all persons	Primarily people of Japanese ancestry.
May be excluded	Forcibly evicted from one's home.
Native American aliens	Renunciants, or citizens who, under pressure, renounced U.S. citizenship.
Assembly center	Temporary detention facility.
Relocation center	American concentration camp, incarceration camp, illegal detention center. Inmates held here were referred to as incarcerees.
Internment center	Reserve for DOJ or Army camp holding alien enemies under Alien Enemies Act 1798. [2]

---

2. National JACL Power of Words II Committee. *Power of Words Handbook: Euphemisms and Preferred Terminology.* Japanese American Citizens League, (April 2013) 14.

In 1988, the Civil Liberties Act was signed into law by then President Reagan. The law allowed approximately 80,000 ex-internees alive at that time to receive $20,000 per person. The formal payment and apology would begin to bring about reparation and healing for formerly-incarcerated Japanese Americans. For Michi, her work to bring justice continued. She supported railroad workers fired from their jobs and draft resisters who did not sign the loyalty questionnaire and were excluded in the redress. How many countries would attempt to right such a wrong?

Michi Nishiura Weglyn's life exemplifies the bushido code in her determination to do what she could to right a wrong; this is the very embodiment of the meaning of integrity. It was important to her to rectify the injustice inflicted upon herself, Japanese Americans, and Japanese who were incarcerated during World War II. She dedicated most of her adult life to this cause through her lengthy research in writing her book, speaking, and being an advocate for those who did not speak up for themselves. Michi said what she meant, meant what she said, and then did it.

A life lived with integrity—even if it lacks the trappings of fame and fortune—is a shining star in whose light others may follow in the years to come.

—Dennis Waitley

Walter Weglyn passed away in 1995. Michi continued her work, even though her health was declining. She generously shared her time and research through letters and telephone calls to colleagues and friends.

Michi Nishiura Weglyn died of cancer on April 25, 1999, in New York. She did not want a memorial, although she will always be remembered, honored, and loved by many.

In the words of Phil Tajitsu Nash, personal friend and later her literary executor, the reasons he admired and loved Michi were:

- She was always herself

- She lived art

- She savored life

- She aimed high

- She never gave up

- She lived life with purpose

- She told the truth

- She shared her gifts

- She never forgot

- She lived the future

Michi Nishiura Weglyn was a lovely woman with a beautiful heart, full of integrity. She did the right thing by rectifying a grave injustice.

It is my sincere hope that this story
of what happened only a generation ago
may serve as a sobering reminder
to us all that even Constitutions
are not worth the parchment
they are printed on unless vitalized
by a sound and uncorrupted public opinion,
and a leadership of integrity and compassion.

—Michi Nishiura Weglyn

Michi's words are echoed in a quote from the Bainbridge Island Japanese American Community (BIJAC) of Bainbridge Island, Washington:

Nidoto Nai Yoni; "Let it not happen again."

This is the motto and mission of the Bainbridge Island Japanese American Exclusion Memorial. The Bainbridge Island Japanese American community was the first to experience Executive Order 9066. They were forcibly removed from their homes by U.S. soldiers carrying rifles with fixed bayonets, as they boarded a ferry to Seattle, Washington, to an unknown future.

Senator Daniel K. Inouye

Inouye Family Kamon   Medal of Honor

As a leader, you have to not only do the right thing,
but be perceived to be doing the right thing.
A consequence of seeking a leadership position is
being put under intense public scrutiny, being
held to high standards, and enhancing a reputation
that is constantly under threat.

—Jeffery Sonnenfeld and Andrew Ward

The late U.S. Senator from Hawaii, Daniel K. Inouye, is known and respected as the highest-ranking Asian American politician in U.S. history. Before his career as a politician, Inouye demonstrated during World War II the integrity of his character to lead by example. Not content to simply give orders, he earned the respect and admiration of his fellow soldiers through his unselfish acts on the battlefields of Europe. Born in 1924 as the son of Japanese immigrant plantation workers, Inouye encountered prejudice and discrimination and, as a result, dedicated his life to the cause of helping his fellow man.

Inouye wanted to become a doctor after having orthopedic surgery from a wrestling injury. Following his passion, he became a pre-med student, aid station worker, and a Red Cross volunteer. When the United States entered World War II in 1941, his destiny took an entirely different course.

Like other Japanese Americans from Hawaii, Inouye wanted to prove his loyalty to America and serve his country. He left college and volunteered to join the all-nisei 442nd Regimental Combat Team.

Inouye was a platoon leader in the Vosges Mountains in France in 1944. The regiment was engaged for two weeks in an effort to relieve the American Lost Battalion that was surrounded by German forces. While leading an attack, a shot struck Inouye in the chest, but he was saved by two silver dollars in his pocket. These same two silver dollars were carried in his pocket for good luck until they were later lost. He was promoted to second lieutenant for his bravery and leadership.

In the northern Italy campaign, Inouye bravely and skillfully directed his platoon through enemy fire that brought his men within 40 yards of a hostile force near Tuscany. The Gothic Line was a strongpoint along the German fortification, and it was considered the last and most unyielding line of German defense in Italy. During an encounter, he led his platoon within five yards of a machine gun and destroyed this emplacement by personally hurling two grenades into the enemy position. Under fire from a second machine gun, he stood up to continue the assault. He was wounded by a sniper's bullet while an exploding grenade shattered his right arm. Inouye was in intense pain, yet he refused treatment and directed his platoon until his men advanced through the difficult resistance. He displayed true leadership by considering the safety of his platoon before himself. Inouye continued fighting until he was wounded in the leg, tumbled down a ridge, and collapsed from blood loss.

The men from his platoon were concerned about Inouye's condition. However, after regaining consciousness, he instructed them to return to their position, and stated, "Nobody called off the war!" He was not concerned about his personal condition because he was focused on the greater need of victory for all. He was taken to a field hospital where the doctors grew dubious about his condition. Inouye convinced them to operate, and his right arm was amputated, saving his life but ending his dream of becoming a doctor. In 1947, he was honorably discharged as a captain.

For his service in the U.S. Army, Inouye was the recipient of the following awards:

- Two Purple Hearts

- Bronze Star Medal

- Distinguished Service Cross, which was upgraded to Medal of Honor by President Clinton in 2000

- Presidential Medal of Freedom awarded posthumously in 2013

Citing from *Lost & Found: Reclaiming the Japanese American Incarceration*, three noncombat-related incidents changed Inouye's life forever as stated on March 9, 1998, at a meeting with New York Jewish and Japanese American leaders:

> *First, after the nation of Japan bombed Pearl Harbor, he and all nisei were reclassified 4-C, which designated them enemy aliens, an accusation that gravely insulted him then and now.* [3]

Inouye wondered how he could have been considered an enemy alien when he was an upright American citizen born and raised in Hawaii. Being of Japanese heritage, this proved to be extremely insulting to him.

---

3. Ishizuka, Karen L. *Lost & Found: Reclaiming the Japanese American Incarceration,* (Urbana and Chicago: University of Illinois Press, 2006) 164.

Second, after having volunteered for the segregated,
all-Japanese American 442ⁿᵈ Regimental Combat
Team, he and other nisei soldiers visited Rohwer,
one of the ten American concentration camps. [4]

After Inouye and the other nisei soldiers from Hawaii had visited Rohwer, the ride back to the barracks was silent and sobering. They had a better understanding of the discrimination that the mainland niseis faced. He wondered if he would have volunteered if he were in their place.

Third, while in the hospital in Atlantic
City in June 1945, recuperating from his battlefield
wounds, he met a fellow Japanese American soldier
who served in the 522ⁿᵈ Field Artillery Battalion,
which liberated one of the satellite camps of Dachau.
This soldier told Inouye first hand of the horrors
he encountered there. [5]

The conversation had a profound effect on Inouye. As a senator, he introduced a bill to repeal Title II of the Emergency Detention Act of 1950 some 20 years later. The Act had the authority to construct domestic camps for suspect individuals as a threat to national security; unfortunately, this was the fate of Japanese Americans during World War II.

---

4. Ibid.
5. Ibid.

The senator ended his comments by saying that we—Japanese Americans and American Jews—should be working together, and that together we could prevent the question of who might be next from ever arising. [6]

For many, the misfortune of shattered dreams would have been a debilitating setback. Not for Inouye. His life's goal was always to be of service to others. The loss of his arm was merely an obstacle to overcome, not an excuse to abandon his dream. He returned to college under the G.I. Bill, and graduated from George Washington University Law School. He soon started his political career. This fulfilled his vision of serving his fellow man, simply in a different capacity.

Keep true, never be ashamed
of doing right, decide on what
you think is right and stick to it.

—George Eliot

In his 58 years as a public servant, the late Senator Daniel K. Inouye was never defeated as an elected official. He became President Pro Tempore of the Senate—third in the presidential line of succession and the second-longest serving U.S. Senator in American his-

6. Ibid., 165.

tory, behind only Robert Byrd. During Inouye's distin-guished career, he was dedicated to serving his fellow man, particularly in the cause of equal rights for all Americans, having experienced discrimination himself.

Daniel K. Inouye was a true American hero who served his country until the moment he passed away on December 17, 2012. He was honored and laid in state at the United States Capitol Rotunda, the 31st person and the first Asian American to be given this honor. Inouye's example of integrity under trying conditions is an inspiration to Americans and all who cherish freedom. Daniel K. Inouye, a true American hero, in his last moments befittingly penned, *"Aloha."*

The late Senator Daniel K. Inouye was a true warrior who demonstrated the samurai traits of courage, honor, and integrity, and by serving and protecting. Is there a greater honor? In the midst of your battle, will you face challenges and obstacles with the same spirit as Inouye? If you let honor be your trademark and integrity your calling card, the world will be a better place because of you.

Your reputation and integrity are everything.
Follow through on what you say you're
going to do. Your credibility can only be
built over time, and it is built from the
history of your word and actions.

—Jeffery Sonnenfeld and Andrew Ward

Chapter Three

BENEVOLENCE

仁

JIN

Japanese Kanji
for
Benevolence

Jin

BENEVOLENCE

*You have not lived today until
you have done something for someone
who can never repay you.*

—John Bunyan

Benevolence is the disposition to show respect under all circumstances. It embraces a universal regard toward mankind; a tendency toward good; to be conscious of others' distress with a desire to alleviate it.

The kanji *jin*, benevolence, is comprised of two parts: the character on the left side represents a human, or *nin,* in Japanese, and the character on the right side represents the number two, or *ni,* in Japanese. The two together comprise the ideogram, jin. The kanji literally means "two people." Its meaning is derived from the Chinese ideogram *ren* and the Confucian idea of the essence of being human, or the way two people should treat one another. One who is humane is always in virtuous relationship with other people.

Webster defines benevolence as a disposition to do good, an act of kindness, and a generous gift. The samurai were fierce warriors, yet they demonstrated benevolence toward those they regarded worthy of respect. This principle and virtue set the samurai apart from other warriors of their day.

We live in a fast-paced society with rapidly increasing innovations readily available. Technology is advancing swiftly. Knowledge is increasing at a pace such as the world has never known or experienced. However, despite our increase in technical knowledge, we are still living beings with a heart and soul.

Benevolence is an often-misunderstood term today. The concept of benevolence is a form of respect. It is the idea of providing a hand up rather than a hand out.

A wealthy and wise man doesn't
shake hands with people,
he gives a helping hand.

—Michael Bassey Johnson

The samurai demonstrated benevolence when they defended the weak or allowed a vanquished foe to die an honorable death. In World War II, the U.S. Military Intelligence Service (MIS), comprised entirely of Japanese Americans, interacted with benevolence and compassion to captured Japanese prisoners. Rather than acting harshly, they understood the importance of saving face and befriended their enemies. Their *enemies* were from the land of their parents' birth; this caused both confusion and compassion. During the reconstruction of Japan after World War II, the MIS became the bridge between the Americans and the Japanese. They understood the language and culture, provided a smoother transition, and contributed to a more successful reconstruction.

An act of kindness, especially toward the less fortunate, is good for the soul. It is a gesture that blesses both the giver and receiver. When we sow seeds of goodness, those seeds will come to fruition in our lives, sometimes in unexpected ways.

Kind hearts are better than fair faces.

—Japanese proverb

In America, we are a nation of givers. Many organizations exist to serve others' needs. We give of our hearts by donating time and money to assist others. Much of this is an acknowledgment of our own blessings and a desire to reach out and aid those less fortunate.

Benevolence was developed in the samurai through engaging in artistic endeavors. *Haiku* (Japanese poetry), writing, storytelling, and drawing required exercising the right side of the brain. It was a balance to the left-brain discipline of the martial arts and war strategies.

As a storyteller, I enjoy sharing Japanese folktales with young children. Afterward, I ask questions to see if the children grasped the moral of the story. In one particular tale emphasizing kindness, one boy exclaimed, "Be kind!" Those were his only two words, yet so profound! If we would all be kind, imagine what our world would be like!

Mother Teresa personified the benevolent spirit through her dedication to the poorest of poor in India. It is one thing to have sympathy and pity for the poor, but another to recognize the need and take action to address the condition. In 1979, the Nobel Peace Prize was awarded to Mother Teresa for her devotion to the poor in Calcutta's slums. Being a humble humanitarian, she did not attend the banquet, but rather requested that the money be donated to the poor in India. How many recipients of prestigious awards have been so modest and generous?

Chiune Sugihara wrote exit visas for the Jewish people in Lithuania because of his love for humanity. His samurai upbringing influenced his decision and saved countless lives.

In this chapter, we will discover how two men, Dr. Toshio Inahara and Dr. James Okubo, both gave of their gifts and talents for the good of mankind. Maybe you have experienced benevolence at a critical time in your life. It may even have come from an unexpected source. A kind and selfless deed or an act of kindness speaks volumes. Your actions speak louder than words as you do the right thing all the time.

The conqueror is regarded with awe;
the wise man commands our respect;
but it is only the benevolent man
that wins our affection.

—William Dean Howells

Dr. Toshio Inahara

Inahara Family Kamon

Selfishness leads to nothingness.
Generosity and benevolence leads
to great reward.

—J.W. Lord

Dr. Toshio Inahara has been a personal family friend since he and my father were young. A world-renowned vascular surgeon, Dr. Inahara's regard for mankind was aptly demonstrated, as he helped my mother and both of my brothers in their latter stages of life.

Dr. Toshio Inahara, born in 1921, spent his early life in Tacoma, Washington, where his father was the proprietor of a *kashiya* (Japanese sweets store). When he started school, he had difficulty speaking English but excelled in Math. He enrolled in extracurricular Japanese School, where he learned Japanese language and memorized 1,200 kanji characters.

Father Inahara desired to raise his five sons in the country, so they relocated to rural western Oregon. It was a culture shock to move from the city to the country, where Inahara attended a one-room grade school with 30 students. He enjoyed the country life, fresh food, and playing sports with his brothers. In their favorite samurai game, the brothers carried wooden swords and reenacted famous battles.

After Pearl Harbor, life drastically changed for Japanese Americans. Inahara volunteered for the U.S. Air Force. Though qualified to be an officer, he, like many other Japanese Americans, was classified as 4-C enemy alien and was ineligible to serve. He sought legal counsel to join the service, but he was denied. After this and because of the impending internment, he petitioned the U.S. government to relocate. The Inahara family was granted the atypical permission to move inland to a farm in Vale, Oregon.

He wanted to attend college and was accepted at the University of Wisconsin. It was a difficult decision to leave the family farm, but his younger brothers would take over. He graduated in 1946 with a premedical degree from the University of Wisconsin.

Inahara was accepted to the University of Oregon Medical School in 1946, where he met his future wife, Chizuko. He worked as an extern at St. Vincent's Hospital in Portland, Oregon, during his senior year. He remained at St. Vincent's Hospital after graduation in 1951, taking a residency in general surgery and remained there until 1955.

During his last year of training, Dr. Inahara became interested in vascular surgery, a new field coming into prominence. During his early years as a doctor, he encountered several incidents where he could see the need for improved techniques in this area. An opportunity to go to Massachusetts General Hospital, an affiliate of Harvard Medical School, presented itself. As a fellow, he was fortunate to work with Dr. Robert Linton, a leader in the vascular surgical field. During this time, he worked to develop artificial blood vessels and became a board certified vascular surgeon. He returned to St. Vincent Hospital as the first trained vascular surgeon in the state of Oregon.

In 1972, Dr. Inahara formed a fellowship to teach and train vascular surgery to general surgeons at St.

Vincent Hospital. Training vascular surgeons was spurred by his desire to spread these new techniques in order to help his fellow man. As the director, he trained 20 vascular surgeons not only from the United States, but Honduras, Australia, and Ireland as well. Dr. Inahara's aspiration to train his students to be the best was demonstrated in his personal dedication to each individual student over the one-year training period.

His willingness to generously give of his time and knowledge helped not only the whole world but my family. An example of his generosity occurred in 2003 when my younger brother, Dan Tsugawa, was diagnosed with thymus cancer at the age of 46. The medical staff at Southwest Medical Center in Vancouver, Washington recommended that they perform chemotherapy as soon as possible, although they were not familiar with the effects of this treatment on his condition, or of the outcome.

Uncomfortable with the protocol, Dan contacted Dr. Inahara for a second opinion. Although retired, Dr. Inahara studied Dan's CAT scans, biopsies, and reports as if he were currently practicing medicine. Dr. Inahara took his case to a study group of 30-40 doctors who met at Providence St. Vincent Medical Center in Portland, Oregon. It was fortunate that thoracic surgeon, Dr. Anthony Funari, was one of the members. A surgical approach addressing the cancer was recommended. As a benevolent gesture, Dr. Inahara was in the operating room during the surgical procedure. The surgery was successful, and Dan's life was extended.

Dr. Inahara, together with another vascular surgeon and a business partner, patented a carotid shunt in 1982, which was manufactured in 1984. It is an intricate and vital medical device that he described as:

> *One of the requirements of vascular surgery is*
> *to shunt the circulation while you're working*
> *on the vessel because you're opening the vessel,*
> *but you don't want to stop the circulation.*
> *The lumen (tube) has balloons on either*
> *end that occludes the artery while the blood*
> *is running through the tube. A balloon,*
> *rather than a tourniquet, was used to make*
> *the operation safer and more thorough.*

The medical devices were named Inahara-Pruitt (shorter shunt) and Pruitt-Inahara (longer shunt). The company has since been sold, and the device is still being manufactured and successfully used in vascular surgeries.

Dr. Inahara's invention, the Inahara-Pruitt shunt, would be extremely advantageous for my younger sister, Karen Tsugawa. She suffered multiple brain aneurisms and as a result had two emergency surgeries in 2000. Because of Dr. Inahara's invention, my sister benefited from two successful surgeries and gained a better quality of life.

Dr. Inahara retired as a physician yet he continues to live an active life. On Dad's berry farm, he picks his own strawberries. He also prepares and cooks Japanese meals for Dad. He enjoys traveling and recently retired from snow skiing in his 90s! His generosity extends beyond the sharing of his medical skills. He and his late wife, Chizuko, also graciously donated to the Japanese American National Museum in Los Angeles, California.

Dr. Toshio Inahara is an exemplary example of a physician who took the Hippocratic Oath to heart. Like the samurai, his desire to do good was his deed. He mentored future vascular surgeons, advised family friends, and improved the quality of life for patients; his work continues to have an impact, even into the future. The world is a better place because of one man, Dr. Toshio Inahara, a world-renowned surgeon who cared deeply for his fellow man through his gift of medicine.

Benevolence is the characteristic element of humanity.

—Confucius

Dr. James K. Okubo

Medal of Honor

Dedicated in 2002 at Ft. Lewis, Washington, the Okubo Medical and Dental Complex is a befitting tribute to a courageous and heroic man, Dr. James K. Okubo. The exhibit in the building entrance displays Okubo's life and outstanding service during World War II. Patients and medics in training can view the exhibit, be inspired, and ask themselves if they could respond as gallantly under pressure as Okubo. Would they have enough concern for their fellow man to risk their own lives?

James K. Okubo volunteered to serve as a medic in the all-nisei 442nd Regimental Combat Team of the

U.S. Army. He literally risked his life under enemy fire to rescue and treat fellow wounded soldiers in France. For his bravery, he was awarded the Silver Star – the U.S. Army's third highest decoration.

In 2000, President Clinton upgraded that Silver Star to the Medal of Honor. The citation explains:

Technician Fifth Grade James K. Okubo distinguished himself by extraordinary heroism in action on 28 and 29 October and 4 November 1944, in the Foret Domaniale de Champ, near Biffontaine, eastern France. On 28 October, under strong enemy fire coming from behind mine fields and roadblocks, Technician Fifth Grade Okubo, a medic, crawled 150 yards to within 40 yards of the enemy lines. Two grenades were thrown at him while he left his last covered position to carry back wounded comrades. Under constant barrages of enemy small arms and machine gun fire, he treated 17 men on 28 October and eight more men on 29 October. On 4 November, Technician Fifth Grade Okubo ran 75 yards under grazing machine gun fire and, while exposed to hostile fire directed at him, evacuated and treated a seriously wounded crewman from a burning tank, who otherwise would have died. Technician Fifth Grade James K. Okubo's extraordinary heroism and devotion to duty are in keeping with the highest traditions of military service and reflect great credit on him, his unit, and the United States Army.

After World War II, Okubo graduated from dental school, married, and raised a family in Detroit, Michigan. He tragically died in a car accident at the age of 47 in January 1967. Little did his family know about his heroic World War II service on the frontline until the year 2000, when Okubo's Silver Star was upgraded, and he was awarded the Medal of Honor posthumously. Dr. James K. Okubo demonstrated benevolence and compassion by risking his life to save others. Is there any greater sacrifice?

Every act, every deed of justice and mercy and benevolence, makes heavenly music in Heaven.

—Ellen G. White

Chapter Four

RESPECT

礼

REI

Japanese Kanji
for
Respect

Rei

RESPECT

Respect for ourselves guides our morals;
respect for others guides our manners.

—Laurence Sterne

The character *rei* actually means rite or ceremony, but in a broader sense, it means respect. It is an expression of action toward others, a fundamental politeness that is often related to the character for benevolence, jin. Rei can even be translated as having to do with morality and politeness shown in social behavior. Like most of the characteristics of bushido, it is expressed in both word and deed.

If we look at the meaning of respect found in Webster's dictionary, we find that the definition is to feel or show honor or esteem; hold in high regard; to treat with deference or dutiful regard.

In Japanese culture, the expression of respect is most noticeably demonstrated in social etiquette. Respect was a way of life for the samurai. It delineated both rank and social standing in a society governed by a very rigid class system. The samurai believed it would be better to lose one's life than to be impolite or disrespectful. Proper respect was an expectation in both word and deed. As true warriors, this respect was extended not only to their superiors, but even to their enemies. Today, respect is an important part of our human interactions that is often in short supply.

Many of the universal values and virtues that contribute to a good society affirm our human dignity. These values are often expressed in respect for the individual:

Without feelings of respect,
what is there to distinguish
men from beasts?

—Confucius

Those who understand the role respect plays in both social and business environs can instill trust and motivation in others. We will discuss respect in this chapter as it relates to Japanese etiquette and social customs. Respect was also displayed by members of the Military Intelligence Service (MIS) when they treated their enemies with kindness and dignity.

Respect is not only a gesture offered to others; it is an important reflection of our own self-worth. Those who know and respect their own strengths and weaknesses are more able to recognize and respect what they see in others.

Self-control is the chief element
in self-respect, and self-respect
is the chief element in courage.

—Thucydides

Japanese Etiquette

Laws control the lesser man.
Right conduct controls the greater.

—Mark Twain

According to the 2013 census, Japan has a population of approximately 127 million people living in an area similar in size to the state of Montana. The census also states that Montana, with a population of 1,015,165 people, has a population density of 6.5 people per square mile, while in Japan, it is 873! Japan is known throughout the world as a safe and pleasant place to visit because of its ancient social structure. Adherence to proper etiquette promotes peace and harmony in one of the most densely populated countries in the world. *Wa,* usually translated as harmony, is a guiding principle in Japanese society, family, and business structure.

The Japanese etiquette code is essential in society and governs the lives of Japanese. In pre-industrial Japan, Japanese adhered to a prescribed code of manners shaping every facet of their lives. This became part of their unique personality. A violation of etiquette meant losing one's place in life. The first foreigners to Japan were amazed at the level of civility and etiquette of Japanese, taking note of their remarkable customs that promoted peace and harmony. Proper etiquette is passed down from one generation to the next and is a defining trait of the Japanese.

To any foreigner, bowing is the form of respect most widely recognized as a Japanese custom. Children learn to bow properly at a young age. Japanese companies even provide appropriate training of bowing for their employees.

The Japanese hierarchy is significant, and it is imperative to be mindful of one's status as well as age. Greetings are ritualized; it is important to show proper respect and deference based on your social position in comparison to the person being addressed. It is impolite to introduce yourself and more acceptable to be introduced by another person. In Japan, personal connections are of utmost importance.

Whenever two people come together
and their behavior affects one another,
you have etiquette.

—Emily Post

The Japanese are respectful of their elders by showing reverence and honor, a tenet of Confucian ethics. It is common practice for three generations to harmoniously live together with the younger generation(s) showing deference and respect to their elders. Growing up with other Japanese families, my mother taught me to show respect and address my grandmother as *obaasan* and grandfather as *ojiisan*.

Old people are everyone's treasures.

—Japanese Proverb

In business and life, referrals and personal contacts are essential, and part of the fabric of our lives. These relationships are based on honesty and mutual respect.

We have relationships and conduct business with those whom we trust and like. The Japanese business and social culture relies on personal contact. The custom of exchanging *meishi* (business cards) has a protocol: you receive and review the card with much care and take note to deliver a proper comment. Keep the card out while speaking to the person and do not put it in your back pocket or wallet. If you put it in your back pocket, in essence you will be sitting on their face – a major cultural faux pas. Also, it is offensive to write on the business card. Social rules are so ingrained in Japanese society that Japanese people conduct their lives without having to think about these rules.

In Japan, manners are of utmost importance. Children are taught at a young age to be polite, re-spectful, and display good manners. I have firsthand knowledge of this practice growing up with my Japanese mother. All of my brothers and sisters can remember being instructed and reminded by Mother; always display proper manners. She would always say that it was just as easy to use good manners as bad manners, so why not use good manners?

The Japanese school system also reinforces the im-portance of proper manners. School children are in-volved with their lunches from serving to clean up.

In addition, nutrition and social etiquette are taught at their mealtime. I observed a classroom meal in Tokushima, Japan, where my Japanese friend was a teacher. The children were well mannered, orderly, and wasted very little food.

In Japanese society, "*face*" is a mark of personal dignity, and saving face is crucial. Failure to fulfill obligations results in loss of face, which is more than an embarrassment or being insulted. It is a mark of shame. Shame is a loss of respect, and a loss of respect is a loss of dignity, a fate nobody desires.

Respect is sometimes best understood as an appreciation for the individual. It is often expressed in attention to detail, whether in proper table etiquette when eating your food or a listening ear when someone expresses an opinion or idea. Whether in business or daily life, our interactions often revolve around relationships. It is those relationships that often determine our path in life, particularly in Japan.

For anyone wanting to excel, respect must govern the way we live our lives. The samurai were immersed in etiquette protocol and punished for even minor infractions. This was a way of life taught in school and ingrained throughout the martial arts. The Japanese didn't only ingrain how to think, but combined it with purposefully training their bodies to move a certain way until movement was a conditioned response requiring no thought.

The samurai held themselves to a high standard. True warriors showed respect and proper etiquette—even to their enemies. Their strength in battle as well as their dealings with people were regarded as a mark of bushido.

After World War II, Japan's rise in world stature was seen as an economic miracle. Westerners were fascinated with Japanese business practices and studied their means to success. Respect (rei) is a guiding principle and an integral part of the Japanese business culture. It promotes peace, harmony, and conformity, because employees and managers operate in human-oriented circles rather than the linear layers of western society.

Life be not so short but that
there is always time for courtesy.

—Ralph Waldo Emerson

Military Intelligence Service (MIS)

Congressional Gold Medal

Never in military history (because of MIS)
did an army know so much about the enemy
prior to actual engagement.

—Douglas MacArthur
General of the United States Army

In 1972, Executive Order 11652 declassified
military intelligence documents from World War II.
With the release of this information, the United States

Military Intelligence Service (MIS) contributions and accomplishments to World War II victory were finally recognized. The MIS was America's incalculable weapon in the Pacific and one of the best-kept secrets of World War II. The men and women of the Military Intelligence Service trained and served as interrogators, interpreters, translators, radio announcers, and propaganda writers.

> *The nisei (in the MIS) shortened the*
> *Pacific War by two years*
> *and saved possibly a million*
> *American lives.*

—Major General Charles Willoughby,
General MacArthur's Chief of Intelligence

The contribution of the MIS was crucial to the outcome of the war; MIS soldiers participated in every American battle against the Japanese, including the final assaults on Okinawa and Iwo Jima. They served in all military branches: the United States Army, Navy, Marine Corps, and Air Force. They also served with the British, Australian, New Zealand, Canadian, Chinese, and Indian forces fighting the Japanese. The

MIS soldiers fought fiercely against the Japanese in the Pacific similar to the 100th Battalion and the 442nd Regimental Combat Team in Italy and France.

Approximately 6,000 nisei and *kibei (*those born in America but educated in Japan) fought against the land of their parents and ancestors. They served in the MIS as Japanese language translators and linguists during the war. Imagine the heart-wrenching situations the nisei and kibei faced, knowing they could, and did, encounter relatives and classmates as enemies? They honorably demonstrated and proved their loyalty to a country that discriminated against them and classified them as 4-C enemy aliens. How would you have responded under similar circumstances?

On November 1, 1941, in San Francisco at the Presidio, the U.S. Army secretly opened the Military Intelligence Service Language School (MISLS), only weeks before Japan bombed Pearl Harbor. The first MISLS students came from the Army, but later students were recruited from the American incarceration camps. Especially beneficial were the kibei recruits, because they had a command of the Japanese language and understood the subtle nuances and intentions behind written and spoken Japanese words. Their contribution was invaluable to the Allied war effort.

Saving face is important in the Japanese culture. Questioning the Japanese Americans' integrity and loyalty to the United States was seen as a lack of respect and an affront to their honor. However, this honor and respect would be restored by translating over 18,000 captured documents, including battle plans, maps, diaries, letters, and orders. They also interrogated more than 10,000 Japanese prisoners of war.

The nisei of the MIS understood the concept of honor and respect that was part of their Japanese heritage. By speaking kindly and treating their captives with honor and dignity, they were able to win their trust. Gestures, such as a conversation or song in Japanese or an offered cigarette, helped the MIS linguists develop a bond with these prisoners of war. These simple acts of kindness demonstrated respect for their enemy and allowed the prisoners to maintain their dignity, ultimately providing an environment conducive to the exchange of information.

On August 15, 1945, Emperor Hirohito announced Japan's surrender to the Allies, ending the war in the Pacific. Nisei MIS linguists accompanied General MacArthur when he signed the surrender documents. Through the MIS linguists' understanding of the Japanese culture, the representatives of Japan were allowed to surrender in a respectful manner that retained a sense of honor and dignity.

Over 3,000 MIS soldiers served during the occupation of Japan, and were a communication bridge between the Japanese and American officials; Americans did not speak Japanese and the Japanese did not speak English. The MIS members contributed in civil affairs, intelligence, and military disarmament. More than that, their presence fostered a peaceful and successful relationship between the occupational forces and Japanese. The relationship was enhanced in part due to their knowledge of both cultures and led to an easier transition for a vanquished foe.

While living in Japan, Editor Mike Jenkins heard an interesting World War II story about baseball. In Kobe City, which had been flattened by bombing, the Occupation forces marched in with trucks and jeeps and brought brand new baseball bats and balls. The Japanese people peering out of boarded windows of what was left of their homes were very frightened. They thought that the American soldiers had come to beat them to death with bats because the soldiers were piling bats beside large personnel carriers and other trucks. But when the Americans put on their baseball gloves and catcher's mitts, and started playing ball in the fields and streets outside, the Japanese all came out of their homes and joined them. This is partly the reason baseball is such a huge sport in Japan today.

On a personal note, my father George Tsugawa's two brothers served in the MIS. Henry Tsugawa, the elder brother, served in the MIS overseas. He mentioned that he had bodyguards in the Philippines in the event he was mistaken as being an enemy combatant from Japan. Unfortunately, Henry passed away before he was able to share much about his World War II experiences. Because of the efforts of his youngest brother, Dr. James Tsugawa, Henry was posthumously awarded the Congressional Gold Medal in 2010. Akira Tsugawa, the younger brother, served in the MIS in the United States. Being Japanese, neither Henry nor Akira wanted to attract personal attention, and did not talk about their wartime service. Henry and Akira proudly and courageously served their country. A family friend, Fred Irinaga, aka Uncle Fred, also served in the MIS in the United States. Their wartime service helped restore the respect and honor that younger Japanese American generations enjoy today, including me.

*These guys are the reason why our families
are here and we are so successful,
we are so fortunate, so happy and blessed,
is because of them.*

—Tamlyn Tomita, Actress

In April 2000, the Military Intelligence Service was awarded the highest honor given to a U.S. military unit—the Presidential Unit Citation—over 50 years after World War II ended. In October 2010, the Congressional Gold Medal was awarded to the 6,000 Japanese Americans who served during the war in the MIS. Their outstanding loyalty, sacrifice, and service to the United States was at last recognized, although posthumously for most.

The United States demonstrated its greatness and humility by recognizing and rectifying this oversight. The Presidential Unit Citation awarded the MIS was an acknowledgment and a sign of respect for the men and women who served their country honorably during a difficult period in our history. How many countries in the world would try to resolve such a shortcoming?

Duty, Honor, Country. Those three hallowed words reverently dictate what you ought to be, what you can be, what you will be.

—Douglas MacArthur

Chapter Five

HONESTY

誠

MAKOTO

Japanese Kanji
for
Honesty

Makoto

HONESTY

*Honesty is the first chapter
of the book of wisdom.*

—Thomas Jefferson

L ike many kanji in the Japanese language, *makoto* is comprised of two parts. The character on the left, makoto, is translated *to speak*, and depicts a mouth producing words. On the right, the character *sei* means to accomplish, succeed and to refer to our actions. For the samurai, his words dictated his actions. There was no need to affirm his words by a gesture such as a handshake. Once spoken, the commitment was assured. Thus, honesty becomes the fusion of words and deeds; words = actions.

Webster defines honesty as fairness and straightforwardness of conduct and adherence to the facts, sincerity.

For the samurai, speaking and doing were one and the same. When a samurai said he would execute an action, it was considered done. A true samurai was honest, sincere, truthful, and above reproach to both those above and below him; including all who were in his care. The lives in the samurai's care depended on him. The samurai warrior lived by truth, and there was no place for dishonesty or insincerity.

The samurai developed his credibility through trust. If he breached this trust, he failed his honor. That usually meant death, because death would be the only way to right a breach of honor. For the Western mind, this concept may be foreign and challenging to understand; it was a way of life for the samurai.

In Japan today, this is why there are many spoken agreements that are just as legal as written agreements. Western society depends on written and sealed documents, while the Japanese society depends largely on word-of-mouth agreements. Trust is always assumed, and it cannot be breached without dishonoring the family...even the entire village, town, or company.

Honesty is the best policy. If I
lose mine honor, I lose myself.

—William Shakespeare

Notice again in this quotation the connection to the idea of honor. Much can be learned from this simple statement. Those who desire to excel in their endeavors need to embrace this most important concept.

Honesty is the best policy, but is honesty an easy policy? Does the price of losing your honor and self-worth merit compromising? Conceivably, there are positive and negative effects of being honest. The negative effects of honesty are rejection, hostility, and hurt feelings. How often do we find it more convenient to deviate from the truth? The ultimate effects of being honest are much more far reaching—they bring peace of mind and a positive sense of self-worth.

Honesty begins with your thoughts. When you think honestly and truthfully, your actions follow. As a Transition Counselor at the Washington State Mission Creek Correction Center for Women (MCCCW), I can comment on their thought patterns that resulted in these women's current incarceration. In order to change their situation, their thoughts and lives need to change. When you change your thoughts, you change your life. It all begins with what goes on between your two ears. Every action and spoken word commences with your thoughts.

It takes courage to be honest. Honesty is considered a part of your foundation and moral character. Do you desire your foundation to be solid, like concrete? As the winds of life toss you to and fro, do you want to be on solid ground or sinking sand?

The samurai followed and adhered to all the virtues of bushido. He was not at liberty to select those parts he liked, but was obligated to practice all aspects of bushido in his everyday life. If the samurai did not follow the bushido code, he was not a samurai. He had to live and breathe these principles and be prepared to do the right thing at all costs.

Thomas Jefferson wrote, *"Honesty is the first chapter in the book of wisdom."* Solomon is considered one of the wisest and wealthiest men of all times. In his early life, Solomon sought wisdom above all, and God granted him both wisdom and riches.

The samurai virtue of honesty is still evident in Japan today as we will discuss in the next chapter. After the tsunami on March 11, 2011 struck the northeast coast of Japan, there was little looting and virtually zero rioting. In fact, the Japanese people returned millions of dollars to their rightful owners in the form of cash and valuables.

We will also discuss the story about Uwajimaya, a destination Asian good store in the Pacific Northwest, and its beginning in the back of a truck. By adhering to the bushido code, Uwajimaya has become an information specialist on Asian culture, a nationally recognized name in the supermarket industry and was *Seattle Business Magazine's* 2013 Large Firms Family Business Winner. Honesty is a hallmark of most successful businesses. For the Japanese immigrants, this was a foundational principle they brought with them from Japan.

As you conduct your life, consider:

- Are my words and actions aligned?

- Is a 'white lie' really white or is there a cost that will eventually require payment?

- Are my actions conducive to the business or relationship I desire in my life?

When you do the right thing, success it will bring!

—Arvee Robinson

2011 Tohoku Earthquake and Tsunami

Honesty and integrity are absolutely
essential for success in life – all areas of life.
The good news is anyone can develop both
honesty and integrity.

—Zig Ziglar

Los Angeles Times journalists Tom Miyagawa Coulton and John M. Glionna wrote: "Altruism and honesty among different cultures are difficult to measure and compare, but in 2003 a University of Michigan Law School professor conducted what he called a comparative study on recovering lost property in the United States and Japan.

The professor, Mark West, left 20 wallets on the street in Tokyo and 20 in New York, each containing the equivalent of $20. In New York, he said, six wallets were returned with the cash intact and two were brought back empty. In Tokyo, finders returned 17 of 20 wallets, all with the cash intact, and all but one waived the right to claim the money if the owner wasn't found." [7]

The world was shocked by the devastation of the earthquake and tsunami that struck northeast Japan on March 11, 2011. The loss of property and human life was hard to imagine. For some, the response from the Japanese people was even harder to imagine. Instead of looting and pilfering amidst the ruins, the world witnessed calm, cooperation, and order that focused on helping one another. People organized to help retrieve and return belongings and mementos to individuals and families devastated by the tragedy. Did you witness this in New Orleans after Hurricane Katrina or in New York after Hurricane Sandy? What is there in the Japanese character that made their response so different?

From an early age, Japanese children are taught the virtue of honesty. There is an emphasis on its importance not only to the individual and family, but also to

---

7. Coulton, Tom Miyagawa and Glionna, John M., *Los Angeles Times*, September 22, 2011.

society as a whole. The significance of their individual actions is taught to the children and supported by Japanese society. It is instilled into their character how far beyond themselves their actions affect and reflect others. On a child's first trip to the police station, he/she will be returning a *lost* coin to the officer. Japanese society and government reinforce honesty.

This concept of honesty and shared responsibility is part of the Japanese educational system. School children are taught to perform certain school cleaning tasks and are responsible for serving lunch meals to their fellow classmates.

This code of honesty continued to guide Japanese citizens in the earthquake and tsunami aftermath that destroyed the region of Tohoku. In August 2011, five months after the devastation, officials reported more than 5,700 safes and wallets were given to authorities. In addition, Japan's National Police Agency reported that most of the antiques, gold, cash, and other valuables had been returned to their owners. The amount was a staggering $78 million, with over $30 million in cash from the recovered safes and wallets. According to Ryuji Ito, Professor Emeritus at Yokohama City University: "…the fact that a hefty 2.3 billion *yen* (Japanese basic monetary unit) in cash has been returned to its owners shows the high level of ethical awareness in the Japanese people."

The BBC News also reported:

An anonymous donor in Japan has left 10m yen
($131,000; £83,000) to charity by dumping
it in a public toilet.

The money was found with a letter saying
it should be donated to victims of the earthquake
and tsunami that hit Japan in March.

The neatly wrapped bills were found in a
plastic shopping bag in a toilet for disabled
people in the city hall of Sakado in the Tokyo suburbs.
The note read: I am all alone and have no
use for the money.
The City Hall said it would hand the money to
the Red Cross if it was not reclaimed
within three months.

City officials said the anonymous donor
had slipped in and out unnoticed.

The BBC's Roland Buerk in Tokyo says the
earthquake and tsunami that devastated
north-eastern coastal areas in March has
brought out striking examples of generosity
and honesty. [8]

---

8. *BBC News-Asia Pacific*. (September 29, 2011) http://www.bbc.co.uk/news/world-asia-pacific-15110090 par. 1-6.

The above is an example of the generosity and honesty of the Japanese people.

The tsunami's destruction robbed many of any form of personal identification. Without personal identity, how do you make transactions for the necessities of life? Fortunately, a family registry has been maintained for hundreds of years in Japan. But how do you obtain this personal identification without opening the doors to fraud and identity theft? Government officials were convinced the strong moral character of the Japanese society would prevail, and this would not be a problem. So assured were officials of individual honesty that the Japanese postal system offered banking services to evacuation centers, giving money to people without identification.

Honesty is a mindset that reflects the overall character of an individual or a country. Japan is one of the safest countries in the world. The streets are safe to walk at night. I witnessed grade school children in Kyoto walking down the streets and riding busses and trains unaccompanied, even after dark—a way of life foreign to most other parts of the world.

As a tourist, I experienced and benefitted from several incidents of the honesty of Japanese citizens. While shopping, I accidentally left behind items at a store and also at a flea market. I returned to find them untouched. A Japanese student friend who briefly lived in our area entrusted his Honda vehicle to us to repair and sell for him. When we visited Japan, we sent a letter with 120,000 yen (approximately $1,200 USD) to his residence. You can imagine our hesitancy, but the recipient and the post office assured us that it was perfectly safe. Sure enough, the money arrived safely! Would you ever consider sending money through the postal system where you live? Japan is one of the safest countries in the world because of the moral and ethical character instilled by the bushido code.

The city of Kyoto, inhabited by over 3,000,000 people, is our choice travel destination. I feel safe walking the streets of northern Kyoto alone at night without worrying about the threat of being robbed or assaulted. It is my favorite city in the world because it is inhabited by an honest population and blessed with rich cultural assets.

Japan's low crime rate has been attributed to their homogenous population, strong family ties, and their group mentality. Another factor here is the emphasis on honesty and how it relates to that group mentality. The Japanese think in terms of how their actions will affect not only themselves, but also others. It's as if all of Japan lives in the zone of Zen thinking. There's no dissent, and if there is, it is organized in such a way that does not bring about disharmony. Even the act of disagreeing is done in a polite manner. Trust is essential—this is why criminal activity is seen more as a deviation from what is the norm for the culture. Honesty builds trust, trust builds relationships, and relationships build almost everything else!

Let's live helping each other in this world.

—Japanese proverb

If your desire is to lead a productive life or build a reputable business, then start with honesty with your customers, vendors, employees, family, friends, and yourself.

God lives in an honest heart.

—Japanese proverb

Uwajimaya

Moriguchi Family Kamon

A tradition of good taste since 1928

From the back of a truck, Fujimatsu Moriguchi started his business by selling homemade fishcakes and other Japanese staples to Japanese logging, fishing, and railroad laborers in the Puget Sound area in 1928. It was the humble beginning of Uwajimaya, a destination store in Seattle's International District and *Seattle Business Magazine's* 2013 Large Firms Family Business Winner. Uwajimaya was named after the Japanese town, Uwajima, where Moriguchi learned to make fishcakes and other Japanese delicacies. The word, *ya,* is Japanese for store, and is added to business names.

Fujimatsu Moriguchi and his wife Sadako operated their business in Tacoma, Washington until World War II broke out. The Moriguchi family, including their children, was relocated to Tule Lake War Relocation Center in California where they resided for the duration of the war.

After World War II, the Moriguchis started over at square one, relocating to Seattle and re-opening Uwajimaya in Seattle's Japantown, only two blocks away from the current Uwajimaya Village. Uwajimaya was a retail establishment, fishcake manufacturer, and an importer of food and gift items from Japan.

The 1962 World's Fair was hosted in Seattle, Washington. Moriguchi seized upon this opportunity and operated a small kiosk to display and sell Japanese products. The opening was pivotal and enabled Moriguchi to reach out, educate, and sell to non-Japanese clientele. Uwajimaya offered delicacies, gifts, and food from Japan, opening new doors for the company's success.

When Mr. Moriguchi passed away in the summer of 1962, his four sons took over management. Fortunately, he modeled and taught his family the Japanese work ethic, and so the business continued to grow. Uwajimaya expanded its client and product base to include a wider population and other Asian countries.

In 1970, Uwajimaya moved into its new signature store of 20,000 square feet, and then eight years later, added 16,000 square feet to accommodate its expanding business. Uwajimaya was now the largest Japanese supermarket in the Northwest, and it featured Asian groceries, a delicatessen, live fish tanks, and an extensive gift and dry goods department—years ahead of their time while setting a high standard.

To accommodate Seattle Eastside's growing population in 1978, Uwajimaya opened a retail store in Bellevue, Washington. The third location was added in 1997 in Beaverton, Oregon, a suburb of Portland, Oregon.

Business continued to thrive, and by the year 2000, the Seattle Uwajimaya store built and moved its new home one block south in the heart of Seattle's International District. The new flagship store, Uwajimaya Village, occupies 66,000 square feet and is substantially larger than the previous location. Uwajimaya Village includes Seattle Uwajimaya Asian Food and Gift Market; Kinokuniya, the comprehensive Japanese bookstore; Chase Bank; an extensive Asian food court; and other personal services. Above the store is a 176-unit apartment complex in which residents benefit from the comprehensive retail and service vendors below.

In 2002, Uwajimaya celebrated its 75th anniversary in the new location. Unfortunately, that same year the matriarch, Sadako Moriguchi, passed away at the age of 94. She left behind a legacy and the resilience of the Moriguchi family, who continued to expand the business. The Moriguchis continue to manage Uwajimaya stores and the wholesale food division, with over 400 employees and their $110 million-a-year business.

When I shop at Uwajimaya, I am certain to find Asian ingredients, kitchen accoutrements, and gifts that I am searching for. As in Japan, honesty, customer service, and cleanliness are a high priority at Uwajimaya.

The days of small beginnings on the back of a truck propelled Uwajimaya to become a destination store, an information specialist on Asian culture, and a nationally recognized name in the supermarket industry. From the Uwajimaya website:

> *"Our primary motivation for what we do is
> you, our customer. For this reason,
> it is important for us to deliver
> exceptional service, share our knowledge
> and expertise and be a leader in innovation.
> We celebrate and welcome the diversity
> of our customers and community
> by creating a comfortable, fun
> and unique shopping experience."*

Umajimaya is an exemplary model to follow; from the back of a truck to becoming the nationally-recognized destination store of Asian goods. The Moriguchis are a true American success story of an immigrant family that overcame obstacles, triumphed, and is flourishing. The Moriguchi family has practiced the bushido code in their business and lives…and the legacy continues.

Uwajimaya – always in good taste, always.

Chapter Six

HONOR

誉

MEIYO

Japanese Kanji
for
Honor

Meiyo

HONOR

Life is for one generation;
a good name is forever.

—Japanese Proverb

The first kanji for the Japanese word translated as honor in English is *mei,* meaning reputation. The second kanji is *yo,* which means to praise or admire. The Japanese word *meiyo* (honor in English) literally means to have an admired or praiseworthy reputation.

Merriam-Webster defines honor as a good name or public esteem, (reputation), a showing of merited respect (recognition), a keen sense of ethical conduct (integrity). This is the foundational essence of the Way of the Warrior. Bushido is a code of integrity that brings respect. Perhaps no other characteristic is more influential in Japanese culture than that of one's sacred honor. From bowing when greeting, to presenting business cards, to conducting one's life as an expression to preserve family reputation, honor is infused in the Japanese society.

The samurai lived by the code of honor and refused to compromise because it was a reflection of not only his character, but also his lord, his clan, his family, and his future generations. In feudal Japan, honor was considered a sacred duty by the samurai, and he would rather choose death than surrender or bring shame to his lord or family. The samurai held themselves to high standards, knowing their words and actions were a reflection beyond themselves. Honor is the cord that binds the code of bushido together. Honor is adherence to principles considered righteous.

What is left when honor is lost?

—Publilius Syrus

The Declaration of Independence was signed and adopted on July 4, 1776 by 56 patriots who pledged their lives, fortunes, and sacred honor. Notice that of the three items, *sacred honor*, is the only one that is a principle. Honor was equivalent to their life or their fortune. These men, like the samurai, were willing to give their all for a principle—a praiseworthy reputation. They risked everything, including their lives.

Why should honor be held in such a high regard? Perhaps the answer is found in a line from the movie *Gladiator*: *"What we do in life echoes in eternity."* An echo is a reflection of sound waves. Our reputation, our honor, is a reflection of who we are and what we stand for.

Whether in your personal or business life, the reputation you develop is far more valuable than the size of your bank account or a prestigious location. It defines your integrity and can be the key that unlocks the door to opportunity. Guard your good name. Instill in your family and employees the importance of an honorable reputation, as it will lead you into your future.

In this chapter, we will discuss honor through the life of Saigo Takamori, who was one of the most influential samurai in Japan during the 19th century. He lived in the period known as the Meiji Restoration, a time of great turmoil in Japan. This era saw the end of

the samurai rule and the advancement of modernization. However, the principles that had guided Japan
for nearly 700 years would be the foundation on which
a modern society would be built.

The military shogun was locked in a political battle
with factions seeking to restore the power of the
Imperial Court and Emperor. Takamori strove to
maintain the samurai ways against the onslaught of
Western influence and modernization. Rather than
surrender his way of life, he chose to adhere to the
samurai principle of death before dishonor. Saigo
Takamori was a man of principle, and he is recognized
as the last samurai.

Honor is a significant principle in the Japanese
character. Much humiliation was inflicted on the
Japanese American population living on the west
coast of the United States after the bombing of Pearl
Harbor. Many had family living in Japan; some had
been educated in Japan. Most lost their property and
spent time behind barbed wire; this was an assault on
their pride...and most of all, their honor.

In this chapter, we will also discuss the life of Roy
Matsumoto, whose family was divided by World War
II. He was a member of the Military Intelligence
Service (MIS) and used his Japanese linguistic skill to

assist the U.S. military efforts in World War II. He acted honorably and considered the good of all even when the decisions were so personal.

As a sansei, I was taught to work hard, study diligently and exemplify good citizenship. By my actions, I would bring honor to not only my family and me, but also the entire Japanese community residing in the United States. Much was at stake as a Japanese American after World War II.

One wonders if the idea of honor has lost its place of significance in the 21st century. Leadership requires honor. Without honor, there is no honesty, respect, benevolence, or courage. Without a foundation, it is hard to rise above ground level. Remember *what you do in life echoes in eternity*. Let your echo be one of honor.

Saigo Takamori

A tiger dies and leaves his skin;
A man dies and leaves his name.

—Japanese proverb

Larger than life, Saigo Takamori was a man of un-compromising principle and action. His large stature was extraordinary for 19th century Japan—six feet tall and over 200 pounds. His sharp gaze and intense eyes reflected his unwavering character. A force to be reckoned with, Takamori adhered to the bushido code until his death as a tragic hero. In the end, he was un-willing to compromise, choosing an honorable death rather than betray his principles.

Saigo Takamori was born on January 23, 1828, in the castle town of Kagoshima, which is located on the southwest corner of the southern Japanese island of Kyushu. He was the eldest of seven children born to Saigo Kichibei and Masa, both of samurai lineages. His father was a samurai of *koshogumi* (small name guard) rank, the lowest rank of so-called white-collar samurai. His father struggled financially to support the large and extended family and had to borrow money to make ends meet. These humble beginnings gave the younger Saigo a heart for the less fortunate.

Takamori's career began in 1844 when at 16, he was made a minor official at a rural tax office. Courageously, he submitted petitions proposing measures to lessen peasant distress and denounced corruption. His boldness caught the attention of Lord Shimazu Nariakira, *daimyo* (feudal lord and vassal of the shogun) of the Satsuma prefecture. Lord Nariakira was one of the most important people at the time in Japan, having influence in both the Imperial Court and the Shogunate government. Though of modest rank, Takamori soon became a part of Lord Nariakira's inner circle of retainers. He was dispatched to gather intelligence in the capital city of Edo (present-day Tokyo) during this period.

There was concern among factions of the samurai class that the Tokugawa Shogunate would yield to foreign pressure and growing Western influence. By the 1850s Japan would be forced to open itself and end a long closed period, or *sakoku*, to foreign trade with the arrival of U.S. Commodore Matthew Perry.

In 1858 Takamori was in Kyoto assessing the possibility of an alliance between the Imperial Court and those like himself who were against foreign influence. During this time, Lord Nariakira became ill and died. This sudden death shocked Japan, providing an opportunity for the Tokugawa government to crack down on those showing anti-shogunate leanings, which included Takamori.

Takamori was exiled to Amami Oshima, an island in southern Satsuma, from 1859 to 1862. In 1862, he was pardoned and brought out of exile due to the respect and credibility he attained as the foremost retainer to Lord Nariakira.

Takamori became active in Japanese politics, where his words and actions were sympathetic to the imperialist cause. After he arrived in Osaka, he began meeting with passionate samurai and ronin. These men impressed him, and he later wrote that they were the sort of people 'with whom I would like to die in battle.' Their selfless devotion to the noble cause and request to lead them was appealing to him.

By 1873, the situation in regard to samurai rapidly deteriorated. Takamori resigned all of his government assignments and retreated to a remote village in Kagoshima Prefecture in southern Japan.

After six months, Takamori set up private schools, or *shigakko*, that taught military academics and bushido philosophy. The shigakko was comprised of former officers and soldiers of the Imperial Guard who followed Takamori to Satsuma. By 1876, over 130 schools were operating in Kagoshima Prefecture.

The ratio of samurai to the overall population in Satsuma was nearly one in four, the highest in Japan. The Satsuma samurai had the most formidable reputation and the largest stockpile of weapons of any area. A potential uprising of the Satsuma samurai was not to be taken lightly.

On March 28, 1876, the government banned carrying of swords except for soldiers, police, and officers at state ceremonies. This ban was a major blow to the samurai, who had enjoyed this elite status for centuries. In addition, in August, the samurai's stipend was reduced by 30 percent. Both of these actions were an assault on samurai privileges and identity, and were viewed as a means to undercut their stature.

The government sent warships to Kagoshima to remove weapons from the government arsenal, because they feared a rebellion. This action led to open conflict between the government forces and those samurai loyal to the Imperial household. The protestors approached

Takamori, who was reluctantly persuaded to lead the rebels against the new central government. The Satsuma rebels numbered around 40,000 troops, but were no match for an army of 300,000 equipped with modern weapons. The Satsuma Rebellion was doomed to fail from the beginning. Their number soon dwindled to 400-500, but these samurai were willing to die for their cause. Takamori and his followers made their way to Shiroyama, a hill 107 meters high, where the remaining samurai would make their last stand.

The leader of the government's forces wrote a letter asking Takamori to surrender, but he refused, and spent his last night drinking sake with his men, unwilling to go against his samurai principles. On September 24, 1877, at 3:00 a.m., the government soldiers attacked Shiroyama. Takamori and the remaining samurai used their swords, bows, and arrows, and fought until the bitter end.

With the government victory, the samurai era officially ended. Saigo Takamori lost the battle to preserve the unique samurai tradition and culture, yet he is considered an honorable hero. The principle of honor and the samurai way of life was, to him, greater than his fear of death.

The story of Saigo Takamori provides a very real example of the bushido code as it was embraced and practiced by Japanese samurai. Perhaps this is the reason he is referred to as *The Last Samurai*. From his story, we begin to understand the power behind the concept of honor. Though few are faced with the prospect of defending their principles to the point of death, the esteem given to those who do so is noteworthy. He didn't win, yet he maintains an admirable reputation to this day. Why? Because he was not willing to compromise what he believed. That is what makes leaders. They do not always get the prize, but they know in their heart of hearts that they did the right thing…and that brings respect even from their detractors.

As with Takamori, your reputation and honor extends beyond your present situation; it is something that has been instilled in the bushido code, and it is preserved in the educational and social codes of Japanese society throughout generations.

The Way is a natural way of the Universe,
and to learn it, one must revere Heaven,
love man, and live one's life
from first to last in self-control.

—Saigo Takamori

Japan is a society that strongly adheres to a protocol. Saigo Takamori came from humble beginnings, yet this did not stop him from rising to prominence.

Are there circumstances or situations that are preventing you from stepping into your greatness?

You may be faced with situations in life that require you to defend what you believe. At this time, you need a warrior's resolve. How do you make decisions when your principles are being challenged? Sometimes it may be easier, prudent, or more convenient just to go with the flow and not rock the boat. The right decision may not be easy or popular, but you know deep down inside, you must do what is right, regardless of the outcome. Like Takamori, your principles, honor, and reputation are at stake. He did not separate his personal and professional decisions—they were one. Can this be said about you and your decisions?

How much is your personal or business reputation worth? It is a question perhaps not asked often enough. To the samurai, it was worth everything.

Better to die than to live in shame.

—Japanese proverb

Roy Matsumoto

Matsumoto Kanji   Legion of Merit

The Wakaji Matsumoto family was divided by World War II; two sons fought in the U.S. Army, and three sons fought for the Japanese Imperial Army.

Roy Matsumoto was raised on a farm in Southern California and learned the Japanese work ethic. When he was eight years old, he was sent to Japan to live with his paternal grandparents in Hiroshima, Japan, where he received a Japanese education. The family later joined him but eventually decided to send him back to America to finish his education. This made him a kibei (a Japanese American born in the United States, educated in Japan, and later returned to America).

After graduating from Long Beach Polytechnic High School in 1933, he delivered groceries to Japanese immigrant families in Southern California, and learned many Japanese dialects, idioms, and slang. Little did Matsumoto realize at the time that his Japanese language skills would save many lives and make him a hero.

With the growing tensions from Nazi Europe and from Imperial Japan, the possibility of an America at war surely weighed heavily on young Matsumoto. He had family in both camps. How does one choose loyalties when the consequences become so personal?

When President Franklin D. Roosevelt signed Executive Order 9066 in February 1942, Matsumoto was uprooted temporarily to the relocation center at Santa Anita racetrack in Arcadia, California. He was eventually relocated to the newly established Jerome Relocation Center in Arkansas and faced an extremely difficult time. Times were hard not only for young Matsumoto, but also for all Japanese Americans, many of whom were U.S. citizens living on the West Coast. As mentioned earlier, their loyalty to their homeland was questioned, causing an assault on the honor they held so dear.

At the same time, the United States government was secretly searching for Japanese linguists and recruited Matsumoto from the Jerome incarceration camp. He attended basic training at Camp Shelby, Mississippi, with the 442nd Regimental Combat Team and later the Military Intelligence Language School at Camp Savage, Minnesota. In the fall of 1942, he volunteered for service in the 5307th Composite Unit, Provisional, along with 13 other Nisei linguists. This opportunity was Matsumoto's chance to demonstrate his loyalty to the country he loved and to restore the honor tarnished by the incarceration. Matsumoto and 13 other Japanese Americans joined the clandestine group known as Merrill's Marauders, who gained fame by surviving in the jungles of World War II Burma. This was no ordinary outfit. The Marauders worked deep behind the Japanese lines to gather intelligence, disrupt, and demoralize the enemy on their own turf. Of the 2,700 original Marauders, only 200 survived until the end of hostilities.

Matsumoto's language skills allowed him to intercept and interpret messages on Japanese telephone lines, and he would alert his unit of enemy plans and weapon storage. As an example of his unique abilities, he gleaned the exact Japanese language pronunciation needed to direct an assault from a Japanese field instruction manual. With this knowledge in hand, he bravely stood up with his rifle and gave the Japanese command to charge to an unsuspecting Japanese unit. In response to his command, this unit charged into a waiting ambush and were all killed, while American lives were spared. For his service, Matsumoto was decorated with the Legion of Merit and the Bronze Star.

After the war, Matsumoto was assigned to U.S. Army headquarters in Shanghai, China, to investigate Japanese war crimes. He knew about the catastrophic bombing of Hiroshima, where over 100,000 lives were lost. His family lived in Hiroshima, and his father's photography studio was located less than two blocks from the epicenter. Can you imagine the thoughts that must have entered Matsumoto's mind knowing that he was part of the force that destroyed his own flesh and blood?

I can't imagine being in that kind of situation.
On one hand they are trying to serve
the U.S., but on the other hand,
they have compassion for the people
that are supposedly enemy; which is
their own blood, their own friends and family.

—Jake Shimabukuro
Ukelele Musician

One of Matsumoto's cousins, a soldier in the Japanese Army and prisoner of war in Shanghai, recognized him and shared the unexpected news that the Wakaji Matsumoto family had been spared. They had relocated to the countryside outside of Hiroshima because of a lack of photographic supplies, and in order to maintain military security, photography was forbidden by the government in Hiroshima. Photography had saved their lives! Matsumoto found out from his cousin that one of his brothers who had remained in Japan was also a prisoner of war in Shanghai. He went to the prison to reunite with his brother, where they spoke for several hours. Both his cousin and brother were later released from prison and returned to Japan.

What began as a volunteer service in World War II became a distinguished career in the U.S. Army for Roy Matsumoto. In addition to the Legion of Merit, he was awarded the Combat Infantryman's badge, two Distinguished Unit Citation Ribbons, and five Bronze Stars. In 1993, he was inducted into the U.S. Army Ranger Hall of Fame, and in 1997, he was honored in the Military Intelligence Hall of Fame. In November 2010, Matsumoto was awarded the Congressional Gold Medal along with other nisei veterans from WWII. The

U.S. government is still finding more nisei to award the medal to, now in most cases, posthumously.

Like many other Japanese Americans of his generation, Roy Matsumoto is a living example of what a person of honor is all about. In spite of the situation created by Pearl Harbor and Executive Order 9066, he put those slights aside and rose to the occasion, restoring the honor and good reputation of himself, his family, his generation, and his heritage. Because of the tenacity and dedication of his daughter, Karen Matsumoto, his story is being told. He unassumingly attributes his survival to luck and his fluency in the Japanese language, but we certainly can attribute it in part to his desire to restore the honor of his people.

Honor, a praiseworthy reputation – what is it worth to you?

*No person was ever honored for
what he received. Honor has been
the reward for what he gave.*

—Calvin Coolidge

Chapter Seven

LOYALTY

CHUUGI

Japanese Kanji
for
Loyalty

Chuugi

LOYALTY

Loyalty and devotion lead to bravery.
Bravery leads to the spirit of self-sacrifice.
The spirit of self-sacrifice creates trust
in the power of love.

—Morihei Ueshiba

Chuugi is a somewhat complex character described in two parts. The first (upper) kanji is pronounced *chuu* in Japanese and has the meaning of sincerity or loyalty. The second (lower) kanji is *gi,* which translates as integrity, rectitude, justice, or the correct action. In other words, to do the right thing. The Japanese definition for the combined kanji chuugi is faithful, devoted, true, obedient, and devoted to duty; this is what we translate as loyalty in English.

Webster defines loyalty as the quality, state, or instance of being loyal, and faithfulness or faithful adherence to a person, government, cause, duty, and so on. For the purpose of this book, the quality of loyalty is addressed as a personal attribute or virtue possessed by the samurai and applied to the 21st century warrior.

There is an ancient biblical story about a woman named Naomi, and her daughters-in-law, Ruth and Orpah, who were all widows in the land of Moab during hard times. Naomi sets off on a long journey to her home in Bethlehem. Because of their relationship, Ruth pledges her loyalty to Naomi and journeyed with her. They arrive in Bethlehem in time for the barley harvest when Boaz, Naomi's wealthy relative, meets and falls in love with Ruth. Boaz and Ruth marry, and because of Ruth's loyalty to her mother-in-law, she was able to survive and become the great-grandmother of King David.

Musashi, the famous samurai, set a goal to be the best swordsman in the world. He was loyal to his commitment and achieved that goal. Over his lifetime, he fought and was victorious in over 60 duels. Loyalty is a mindset; it is often associated with dedication to another, be it family, employer, or nation.

However, loyalty applies equally to self. Musashi's dedication and commitment to achieving the goal he individually set are seen as personal loyalty. This is an important point to consider in any goal setting regardless of who is the ultimate benefactor of that goal. When setting goals, you first decide your goal. The more difficult the goal, the more effort you apply toward meeting it. Are the goals realistic? Do I have the fortitude to achieve the goals I set?

Loyalty is a necessary trait for any warrior. To the samurai, loyalty was his sacred duty. It was a measure of his honor. The samurai were devoted and loyal to those under their protection. Faithfulness, steadfastness, and trustworthiness were characteristics of the samurai; the very definition of loyalty.

Like the carpenter, the samurai understood that it would take years to perfect his skills and craft. As the samurai gained competency, he realized that this success would lead to another success as he built his foundation as a warrior. In our fast-paced and modern society, many things are rapid and instantaneous. You can go to the drive-through and have your meal within minutes. Or you could prepare a nutritious meal with thoughtful planning. A consistent and healthy diet leads to success in other areas of your life, so be loyal to and honor yourself.

Henry Ford was faithful and loyal to his dream to create a mass-produced automobile. He set the bar high. If he became discouraged and gave up his goal, he would not have produced the Model T. He certainly faced setbacks, but by remaining loyal to his vision, he accomplished his goal. His determination is expressed in the Japanese word ganbaru...never give up!

Obstacles are those frightful things you see when you take your eyes off your goal.

—Henry Ford

In this chapter, we will discuss the situation of the young nisei soldiers who were determined to prove their loyalty to America during World War II. Eligible Japanese American men volunteered to serve their country even though they and their families were forcibly removed from their homes. They believed that the future of their parents and siblings was dependent upon their service to America, as they fought at its time of need and willingly shed their blood.

In our modern-day society, do you sense a lack of loyalty? Why does it seem our commitments to family, friends, business, country, and even to ourselves is lacking? Have we become so divided, so self-absorbed or alienated, that we have lost our desire to commit to a cause greater than ourselves? Not long ago, employees were loyal to their employer, and an employer was loyal to his employees. What happened?

Chuugi (loyalty in English) is the middle of the heart, sincerity, integrity, rectitude, justice, or right action; to do the right thing. To what do you pledge your loyalty? What dreams and goals are in the middle of your heart? Like the samurai warrior, be loyal to your word, goals, and self, and never give up.

Lack of loyalty is one of the major causes of failure in every walk of life.

—Napoleon Hill

100th/442nd

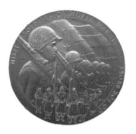

Congressional Gold Medal

Loyalty means nothing unless it has at its heart the absolute principle of self-sacrifice.

—Woodrow T. Wilson

On October 5, 2010, the Congressional Gold Medal was awarded to the Japanese American nisei who had served in the 442nd Regimental Combat Team, the 100th Infantry Battalion, and the Military Intelligence Service during World War II. Prior to the Congressional Gold Medal, the 100th/442nd received:

- 21 Congressional Medals of Honor

- 560 Silver Stars plus 28 Oak Leaf Clusters for a second award for outstanding valor

- 4,000 Bronze Stars plus 1,200 Oak Leaf Clusters for a second award

- 9,486 Purple Hearts

- 52 Distinguished Service Crosses

- 1 Distinguished Service Medal

- 22 Legion of Merit Medals

- 15 Soldiers' Medals

- 2 Meritorious Unit Service Plaques

- 36 Army Commendations

- 87 Division Commendations

- 19 decorations from the Allied Nations

- 9 Presidential Unit Citations

The 100th/442nd suffered the highest casualty rate of any American fighting unit of its size. To this day, they are the the most decorated unit in U.S. military history for its size and length of service. They received over 18,000 individual decorations; their record is without parallel, and these men are without equal. They fought in eight major campaigns, never complained, and there were no AWOL incidents. Instead, there were reported incidents of reverse AWOL when soldiers left medical care to return to battle! These brave men risked everything to prove their loyalty, regain their honor, and restore their rights as citizens of the United States of America. Thus, their befitting regimental motto was *Go for Broke,* from the Japanese word ganbaru or never give up.

The men of the 100th/442nd proved their loyalty with their blood and honorably served the United States of America during World War II. Most of them are gone, but their memories are kept alive by their children, grandchildren, and others, like me. As a sansei, third generation Japanese American, I owe them much gratitude. They paved the way so that future generations of Japanese Americans could experience better lives. I continue to tear up when I write, read, or hear about their stories. They were true samurai and were without equal.

On December 7, 1941, the Japanese Imperial Navy attacked Pearl Harbor. Hawaii was home to a large Japanese American population. In fact, those of Japanese heritage were the ethnic majority. After the attack on December 7th, the United States announced that all ROTC students should report to the Hawaiian Territorial Guard (HTG) for duty. The students were to guard vital installations, bridges, reservoirs, water tanks, and high schools.

Later, officials in Washington D.C. were informed that many of the ROTC students in Hawaii were of Japanese ancestry. They were immediately reclassified as 4-C enemy aliens eligible only for limited service. Undeterred, the former ROTC students petitioned the Governor of Hawaii to affirm their loyalty to the United States. This petition read:

> *We, the undersigned, were members of the Hawaii Territorial Guard until its recent inactivation. We joined the Guard voluntarily with the hope that this was one way to serve our country in her time of need. Needless to say, we were deeply disappointed when we were told that our services in the Guard were no longer needed. Hawaii is our home; the United States, our country. We know but one loyalty and that is to the Stars and Stripes. We wish to do our part as loyal Americans in every way possible and we hereby offer ourselves for whatever service you may see fit to use us.*

In February 1942, ROTC students' wish was granted and they became a labor battalion known as the Varsity Victory Volunteers (VVV). They were attached to Schofield Barracks under the U.S. Army Corps of Engineers, part of the 34th Combat Engineers Regiment.

In December 1942, John J. McCloy, Assistant Secretary of War, visited the VVV in Hawaii. Impressed by what he saw, McCloy advocated that the War Department call for volunteers to form an all-nisei Regiment. Former members of the Hawaii National Guard led the way in the creation of the all-nisei 100th Infantry Battalion in June 1942. The 100th Battalion was the first combat unit exclusively comprised of nisei from Hawaii, with the only non-nisei being commanding officers. The unit comprised 1,432 men serving in the 298th and 299th Regiments of the Hawaii National Guard. The unit was shipped to the U.S. mainland for basic training and wound up at Camp Shelby, Mississippi, where they completed advanced training.

In September 1943, the 100th landed at Salerno, Italy, attached to the 34th Division. They became an elite fighting force, beating the German forces back and opening the road to Rome. The 100th became known as the Purple Heart Battalion because of their high casualty rate and tough fighting skills. They received over 1,000 Purple Hearts.

Meanwhile, on the U.S. mainland, the U.S. Army formed another separate all-nisei unit. This unit was designated the 442nd Regimental Combat Team. The 442nd had three components: the 442nd Infantry Regiment, the 522nd Field Artillery Battalion, and the 223rd Combat Engineer Company. Like the 100th, the 442nd was composed entirely of nisei volunteers from the American incarceration camps and Japanese American soldiers already within the military prior to December 7, 1941 (except for officers). It was ironic that they were classified as 4-C enemy aliens ineligible for the draft. The 442nd, similar to the 100th, trained at Camp Shelby and arrived in Italy in June 1944.

In the same month, the 100th Battalion and the 442nd Regimental Combat Team, were combined and renamed the 100th/442nd Regimental Combat Team (100th/442nd). Initially, the two units did not mesh, but they soon worked out their differences and became a strong force. The men of the 100th/442nd were anxious to prove their devotion and loyalty to their country of birth, the United States of America.

The unit's toughest assignment was to liberate the small town of Bruyeres, France, in October 1944. After three days of brutal battle, the 100th/442nd secured Bruyeres but suffered 1,200 casualties. The plaque in their honor reads:

> *To the men of the 442d RCT, U.S. Army, who*
> *reaffirmed an historic truth here... that loyalty*
> *to one's country is not modified by racial origin.*
> *These Americans, whose ancestors were Japanese,*
> *on October 30, 1944 during the battle of Bruyeres*
> *broke the backbone of the German defenses and*
> *rescued the 141st Infantry Battalion which had*
> *been surrounded by the enemy for four days.*

This plaque was presented by the Japanese American Citizens League - Monument at Bruyeres, France.

Continuing their momentum after only two days of rest, the 100th/442nd was assigned to rescue the Lost Battalion of the 36th Infantry Division. German forces had cut off the Lost Battalion, leaving them isolated, low on supplies, and in danger. After four of the most severe and bloodiest days of battle in World War II, the unit successfully liberated the 211 men of the Lost Batallion at the cost of over 800 casualties.

Their courage, bravery, and loyalty did not go unnoticed. The citizens of Bruyeres still celebrate their liberation and honor the Japanese American soldiers in attendance. There is a street named Rue de 442 in honor of the men of the 442nd who liberated them and sacrificed their lives. The 65th anniversary of their liberation was celebrated in 2010 with a parade and reenactment of the battle. The remaining men of the 442nd were invited and honored with a ceremony.

Two American sisters, Janet and Susan Hardwick, are especially grateful and would not be alive if it were not for rescue of the Lost Battalion by the 442nd. Their father, Sgt. Bill Hardwick, rarely spoke about World War II except for the following story:

> *He always believed the 442nd…were handpicked.*
> *That they were the only ones that could save them*
> *and that there was no success until the 442nd came.*
> *If it weren't for the 442nd, we would never have*
> *known (our dad).*

Sgt. Bill Hardwick desired to locate the soldiers of the 442nd but passed away before he had the chance. The Hardwick sisters fulfilled his wish. Through research and the Internet, they began their search in 2006. This led to their initial contact with surviving members of the 442nd and an emotional encounter with the nisei veterans at Las Vegas in 2007 and 2008. They actually met Arthur Iwasaki (following chapter) at a nisei vet reunion. During a trip to Europe in 2009, they were able to visit the area from which the Lost Battalion was liberated. The sisters met some of the

442nd soldiers who took part in the rescue. This occasion gave them an opportunity to express their appreciation for their courage and sacrifices on behalf of their father. They share this heartwarming story with sincere gratitude amongst their family and friends.

Belmont and Bifontaine also pay tribute to the 100th/442nd; monuments, museums, and streets are named in their honor. In 1962, Texas Governor John Connolly officially declared the 100th/442nd as Honorary Texans.

General Mark Clark specifically requested that the 100th/442nd return to Italy to breach the German Gothic Line. During the night of April 5, 1945, three battalions of the 100th/442nd climbed with their gear up the steep 3,000-foot Mount Folgorito in total darkness. Some men fell to their deaths but made no sound because they did not want to alert the enemy. At 5:00 a.m. after an artillery barrage, they took the German defenders by surprise. In 32 minutes, the 100th/442nd broke through the Gothic Line that prior had withstood 30,000 men and six months of effort by the Allied Army. It is reminiscent of the *ninjas* (feudal Japanese warriors trained in stealth and employed as spies and assassins), as they climbed the mountain in total darkness to launch the surprise attack before the crack of dawn. True samurai spirit and the bushido code: honor, courage, loyalty, and integrity in action!

The German Gothic Line was the key and final offensive that drove the German enemy to the Po Valley, forcing the surrender of the German Army on May 2, 1945, in Italy. Shortly after that on May 8, 1945, Germany surrendered in Western Europe.

The nisei veterans of the 100th/442nd have a unique bond with each other and continue to have reunions and meet to this day. There are organizations dedicated to preserving the memory of the nisei vets who demonstrated loyalty, honor, and courage on the battlefields of World War II. They are modern-day samurai warriors.

The 100th/442nd was the only unit to be personally received upon their return from war by the President of the United States. At the presentation of the Seventh Presidential Unit Citation to the 100th Battalion/442nd Regimental Combat Team on the White House lawn, July 15, 1946, President Harry S. Truman stated so well:

I can't tell you how much I appreciate the
privilege of being able to show you just
how much the United States thinks of what
you have done. You fought not only the enemy,
but you fought prejudice-and won.
Keep up that fight and we will continue to
win-to make this great Republic stand for
what the Constitution says it stands for.

It had been raining that day, and President Truman was advised to cancel the event. President Truman was insistent and said it was a small sacrifice compared to what the men of the 100th/442nd endured.

Some might wonder why the men of the 100th/442nd were so willing to shed its blood for a country that seemingly turned its back on them. The answer is they were Americans…not Japanese Americans, but simply Americans. Their commitment was to defend *their* country as surely as the samurai was committed to defending his lord. It was a commitment to preserving a way of life for future generations and to demonstrate their honor and integrity to a nation that questioned their sincerity.

Loyalty is a commitment; to a cause, to an idea…to a nation. Where do your loyalties lie?

Loyalty and devotion lead to bravery.
Bravery leads to the spirit of self-sacrifice.
The spirit of self-sacrifice creates trust
in the power of love.

—Morihei Ueshiba

Arthur Iwasaki

Iwasaki Kanji   Bronze Star

A close family friend, Arthur Iwasaki, aka Uncle Art, was one of those men of the 100th/442nd. Growing up, our Tsugawa family and the Iwasaki family were like cousins. We were all about the same ages, grew up on the family farms, and understood the value of working hard. Even today, members of both the Tsugawa and Iwasaki families are continuing in the farm and nursery businesses. My father, George Tsugawa, and Arthur Iwasaki attended the same high school and have remained life-long friends. Growing up, I never knew "Uncle Art" was a *hero*.

Iwasaki was drafted into the U.S. Army on March 17, 1942, and was stationed at Ft. McClelland, Alabama for two years. During that time, he was classified as 4-C enemy alien (noncitizen) eligible only to perform menial tasks. This action was somewhat perplexing as well as humiliating for him; he had joined the U.S. Army and was accepted to serve his country. However, later he was relegated to menial tasks because he was Japanese American. He was literally considered and classified as 4-C enemy alien.

In June 1944, Iwasaki became part of the replacement unit for the 442nd because of the high casualty rate. He crossed the Atlantic Ocean, arrived in Marseilles, France, and then traveled to Epinal, France. On October 27th, he was hit by shrapnel on his arm and hand and taken to an aid station in a jeep with two other wounded soldiers. The jeep hit a road mine, and he dragged the two other soldiers to safety even though he was wounded himself. He received a Bronze Star and Purple Heart for his courageous act. Iwasaki took part in breaking the Gothic Line by climbing the steep mountain in the middle of the night to launch the surprise attack on the Germans. While participating in the liberation of Carrère, he was wounded by shrapnel for the second time and received his second

Purple Heart with Oak leaf clusters. He left the Army in November 1945 as Private First Class and returned home to Hillsboro, Oregon.

George Washington, first President of the United States, is quoted:

> *He who wears the Purple Heart has*
> *given of his blood in the defense*
> *of his homeland and shall forever*
> *be revered by his fellow Countrymen.*

The blood of Uncle Art and those like him proved the loyalty and commitment of the Japanese American people to *their* nation, the United States of America.

Today, those of Japanese American heritage are considered part of mainstream America. The prejudices of World War II seem far removed from my generation. We owe this to the soldiers of the 100th/442nd and their willingness to demonstrate their commitment and loyalty during the country's time of need.

In summer 2010, Iwasaki, together with his son and daughter, traveled to France to participate in the celebration at Bruyeres. According to his daughter, Stephanie Iwasaki Sakuye, it was an emotional experience to visit the battlegrounds of France and meet the people who fought alongside her father. The people's reception at Bruyeres and the welcome these veterans and guests received demonstrated appreciation for the many sacrifices the 100th/442nd battalion made to save their town.

Loyalty has a price, but it also has its rewards. My parents' generation paid the price so that my generation could be proud of our Japanese heritage and enjoy our American citizenship.

In October 2010, at the age of 92, Iwasaki traveled with his son and daughter to Washington, D.C. At that memorable time, the Congressional Gold Medal was awarded to the 442nd Regimental Combat Team, the 100th Infantry Battalion, and the nisei serving in the Military Intelligence Service. A grateful nation demonstrated its gratitude by presenting the Congressional Gold Medal to those who served in the 100th/442nd and Military Intelligence Service. Uncle Art was one of those who received this honor.

522nd Field Artillery Battalion

Congressional Gold Medal

The nisei soldiers of the 522nd Field Artillery Battalion of the 442nd had a reputation for being the fastest and most accurate marksmen in the U.S. Army. Many nisei soldiers of the 522nd had backgrounds in science and engineering and a good understanding of mathematics. Thus, they were chosen by General Eisenhower, Commander of the Allied Forces in Europe, to help with the attack on Germany as the war was coming to a close. The 522nd was the only nisei unit to fight in Germany. They became a roving battalion and accomplished every objective of their fifty-two assignments.

A significant engagement occurred around Munich, Germany. On April 29, 1945, the scouts of the 522nd

discovered Kaufering IV Hurlach, a satellite camp of the infamous Dachau concentration camp, and liberated the Jewish prisoners. They were not prepared to witness the horrifying sight of sick, emaciated, and dying prisoners. According to Staff Sgt. George Oiye, *We weren't supposed to be there.* Tom Kono's testimonial at the Museum of Tolerance–Go For Broke Foundation stated:

> *"... when we finally opened the Dachau camp, got in, oh those people were so afraid of us, I guess. You could see the fear in their faces. But eventually, they realized that we were there to liberate them and help them."*

The 522nd continued past the satellite camp and discovered more sub-camps, former prisoners, and evidence of atrocities. The 522nd was assigned to security and set up roadblocks to capture Nazis who were trying to flee. In November 1945, they returned to their homes in the United States to their families who had endured life behind barbed wires.

In the chapter on Chiune Sugihara, I wrote about a young Jewish boy named Solly Ganor. Unfortunately, he and his father were unable to use the exit visas written by Sugihara, and they ended up in one of the Dachau satellite camps. The young Ganor was on a death march and left for dead on the side of the road. Miraculously, Private Clarence Matsumura and three other nisei soldiers from the 522nd pulled him from a snow bank and were able to save his life. At first he thought the soldiers were going to kill him, but he remembered the kind oriental eyes of Sugihara he saw on the faces of the soldiers. Matsumura assured him that he was safe and drove him to receive medical attention.

In 1992, Ganor received a call from historian Eric Saul inviting him to meet with the soldiers who had saved him. The soldiers were being honored by the Knesset in Israel and Ganor was asked to share his remembrances at the meeting. The reunion with the soldiers was very emotional. This meeting opened doors for him to write and share his memories and experiences from the Holocaust. It was the beginning of the release of long-suppressed emotions.

This was an ironic twist of fate. Even though their parents, grandparents, brothers, and sisters were behind barbed wire, they were willing to fight for the country of their birth. The soldiers of the 522nd were true to the samurai code *do the right thing all the time*. They adhered to the principles of honor, loyalty, and commitment to their birth country, the United States of America.

Small in stature, the Japanese Americans who fought in World War II were reminiscent of the samurai warriors of ancient Japan. They proved their loyalty by exemplary service to America in a quiet and professional manner. They overcame suspicion and prejudice and earned the respect and honor for their valiant service. They performed their duties without demanding recognition and avoided attention.

Remember, loyalty is a commitment. There were probably times when you were mistreated, cheated, slandered, or experienced discrimination. This is when your commitment to your principles is tested and determines how real that commitment is. What is your response? Your reaction is the only thing that you can control.

The one thing you can't take away
from me is the way I choose
to respond to what you do to me.
The last of one's freedoms is
to choose one's attitude in any
given circumstance.

—Viktor Frankl

After I had read the book, *Man's Search for Meaning*, my life was never the same; it took on a new meaning because it challenged me to examine what I believed and determined how far I was willing to commit to those principles. The author, Viktor Frankl, suffered and survived starvation, beatings, and other atrocities in the Nazi concentration camps, yet he was determined to live and tell his personal story. In the midst of extreme suffering, he was able to find meaning. The love and loyalty he had for his wife and family sustained him during the horrendous times. The Nazis were able to control his freedom, but not his mind. When he was liberated by the Americans, he learned that his sister was the only other survivor of his family. His book has sold over 10 million copies, was translated into 24 languages, and the Library of Congress considers it one of the top 10 most influential books in the United States.

When we are no longer able
to change a situation – we are
challenged to change ourselves...

—Viktor Frankl

As a Transition Counselor at the Mission Creek Corrections Center for Women, located in the State of Washington, I hear the predicaments and stories of the women in my life skills class. I often question them regarding their commitment to their future. After discussion, I guide the women back to making choices. Everyone has choices. Now that they are incarcerated, what choices and what commitments are they willing to make to create a satisfying life upon release? Will they be loyal to sound principles? How can I help them along their paths? What choices can you make to create the life you were created to live? *Carpe diem!* Seize the day and make your life count!

Strategies are necessary for life. Miyamoto Musashi was considered the greatest swordsman in Japan, and he used the analogy of a carpenter. You must plan, train, and maintain tools to execute your plan and life. In order to succeed, you need to be faithful to yourself and have a strong desire or a *why* for fulfilling your plan. A favorite quote from one of my mentors:

> *When your intention is clear,*
> *the mechanism will appear.*

> **—Brian Klemmer**

In essence, it means loyalty to your goals and your vision will produce the *how* to get it done.

I encourage you to remember the men of the 100th/442nd, Arthur Iwasaki, and Viktor Frankl. When you apply the samurai spirit of *doing the right thing all the time,* facing challenges simply becomes part of life's incredible journey.

Chapter Eight

GANBARU

Japanese Kanji
for
Ganbaru

頑
張
る

Ganbaru

Fall seven times and stand up eight.

—Japanese Proverb

Ganbaru is the Japanese word to stand firm, hold out, and persist. Ganbaru is to do your best, not give up, and hang on—even to the bitter end…go for broke! In the face of demanding odds, continue on tenaciously through tough times. Ganbaru is to commit fully to a task and bring the task to an end. Although ganbaru is not one of the principles of bushido, I believe it is the essence of the samurai spirit.

Ganbaru can also be described as:

- Boldness

- Courage

- Determination

- Firmness

- Focus

- Fortitude

- Motivation

- Perseverance

- Tenacity

Ganbaru is used in situations to express encouragement. The Japanese people use the imperative form of this word, ganbatte to encourage each other in sport and cooperative activities. When facing scholastic exams, students and parents support participants by cheering them on: ganbatte! Do your best, persevere, and commit fully to high achievement.

No matter what circumstance you find yourself in, it is the sincere effort in persevering that is deemed admirable and worthy. The endeavor is evaluated on its own merit. I believe there is always a way to overcome obstacles and succeed; it's not over until it's over.

Ganbaru is a uniquely Japanese word, and it expresses the Japanese people's character. It does not have a direct English definition or translation; it's more a feeling and state of mind. The Chinese and Korean languages both use the characters that make up this word, but they do not express the same meaning.

There is a Japanese proverb, *ishi no ue ni mo san nen*, or to sit on a cold rock for three years until it becomes warm. The proverb aptly expresses the concept of ganbaru by relating the effort needed to succeed in warming the rock. It takes persistence to achieve your goal. Without perseverance and the resolve of a samurai, how do you succeed?

In my personal life, this belief in ganbaru has manifested after sustaining injuries from not one but two rear-end car collisions within a short period of time. I was diagnosed with Traumatic Brain Injury (TBI) and suffered from both physical pain and mental fatigue, unable to perform life's daily tasks. My ability to read tested at a seventh-grade level. However, I was determined to restore my ability to function, so I vowed to fight and persevere until I succeeded!

Most of my life, I have had an aversion to doctors. I remember trying to convince my mother that I was not feeling well on the dreaded day of school immunizations; it didn't work. I attempted to run from the school nurse to avoid receiving *the shot*. The entire TBI ordeal forced me to face my fears as I endured years of doctor appointments and rehabilitation therapy. In fact, I had more doctor and rehabilitation therapy appointments to regain wholeness than in my entire life! I am a baby boomer. From the period of 2005 to 2015, I have endured thousands of appointments to regain my physical and cognitive health. My persistence and tenacity paid off. Because of God's grace and perseverance, I am now a TBI survivor. ***Ganbaru!***

The greatest glory in living
lies not in never falling,
but in rising every time we fall.

—Nelson Mandela

Ganbaru is of significant and central value in Japan. The samurai adhered to the bushido code, and always endeavored to do his best at all costs. Between the years of 1950 and 1980 in postwar Japan, Japanese people worked hard and focused on supporting and rebuilding their country after the destruction of World War II. The slogan, *"Ganbaru Kobe"* was expressed to en-

courage the people of Kobe City to rebuild and recon-
struct their city and lives after the 1995 Great Hanshin
Earthquake. Ganbaru was one of the most commonly
heard expressions after the devastating 2011 Tohoku
earthquake and tsunami. Although faced with great
trials, the prevailing spirit of both the samurai and
ganbaru has lived on in Japan!

Recall when I discussed earlier that Chiune Sugihara
wrote visas to save the lives of the Jewish people facing
annihilation against the orders of the governments of
Japan and Lithuania? He showed ganbaru by continuing to write visas even while his train was departing,
and he threw the signed visas out the window in the
hope that more lives would be saved. Another great
ganbaru example is the late Senator Daniel Inouye,
who courageously continued in battle during World
War II even after his arm was severely wounded, until
he eventually passed out from loss of blood. His arm
was amputated during the battle, ending his dream of
becoming a doctor. His calling then became serving as
a senator for the state of Hawaii until his death.

In this chapter, we discuss the tenacity of my dear
mother, Mable Tsugawa. She persevered and started a
business after the volcanic eruption of Mt. St. Helens
in the 1980s as she neared retirement age. She believed

that anything was possible when you refuse to give up. Mable Tsugawa was a living example of the samurai spirit…integrity, courage, and tenacity…ganbaru!

You would not be given a vision
or dream without the talents
and gifts to make them real.

—Nancy D. Solomon

Mable Tsugawa

Tsugawa Family Kamon

She turned her can'ts into cans
and her dreams into plans.

—Kobi Yamada

What do you do for an encore after you have raised six children and devoted your life to the success of the family farm? Sometimes an empty nest can be a mixed blessing as it was for my mother, Mable Kazuko Taniguchi Tsugawa, a nisei, second-generation Japanese American.

Although Mother was a farmer's wife, she was not born with a green thumb. When the family arrived in rural Woodland, Washington in the 1950s, she attempted gardening for the first time by purchasing bean, corn, and cucumber seeds. She followed the instructions by planting a hill, which she made over 18 inches high! Mother wanted to return the corn seed because it seemed dry and dehydrated. The story became humorous and well-known in their small community. The local people gave her the title of: *the girl from the city!*

The Pacific Northwest was devastated, and everything came to a standstill when Mt. St. Helens erupted on the morning of May 18, 1980. Businesses and roads closed and people relocated when Southwest Washington and beyond was covered in volcanic ash. In only three minutes, the volcano spewed 3.7 billion cubic yards of fiery rocks and volcanic ash into the air. In the aftermath of the eruption there were:

- 150,000 acres devastated

- 57 lives lost

- 250 homes destroyed

- 47 bridges in need of repair

- 15 miles (24 km) of railways destroyed

- 185 miles (298 km) of highway ruined

- millions of trees strewn like matchsticks

- 7,000 big game animals as well as thousands of birds and fish dead

My parents, George and Mable Tsugawa of Woodland, Washington, faced one of the most devastating natural disasters of their lives. It would take courage to continue on when the future was so uncertain.

Have you heard the saying: beauty from ashes? Literally, from the Mt. St. Helens eruption, beauty emerged. Weyerhaeuser Company planted 18,000 seedlings, and some of these trees stand 70 feet tall today. Glass art and ornaments are designed and manufactured from the volcanic ash. Today there is a visitors' center to educate people about the rebuilding of the Mt. St. Helens area. It is a testimony to the restoration and rebuilding following a natural disaster and human tenacity.

Shortly after the Mt. St. Helens disaster, my parents had an opportunity to purchase a nursery business. It was located on I-5 frontage road in southwest Washington in Woodland, not far from Mt. St. Helens. At the time of purchase, it took courage, vision, and imagination to see the possibilities. The property had dilapidated buildings, a history of failure, and uncertainties related to Mt. St. Helens itself.

After purchasing the property, there were some doubts about my parents' newly acquired business.

With sheer determination, my Mother declared, "I can do it!" She had faced challenges in her life with a positive attitude and determination second to none. With little support, she began to embark on her new venture with the courage and resolve of a samurai. Her empty nest dilemma had found a solution.

A worn-down truck accompanied the dilapidated nursery buildings and served as Mother's vehicle when visiting nurseries and purchasing nursery stock. The truck broke down four times on the freeway in the Portland, Oregon, vicinity. It was fortuitous when a family friend happened to be going by and assisted her—three times! After the third rescue, he insisted that Dad purchase Mother a new vehicle!

Mother tirelessly canvassed wholesale nurseries, soliciting advice from the owners in selecting inventory for a successful retail nursery. In the spring of 1981, the nursery opened its doors to the public, an exciting time for the whole family, especially Mother. However, that first week, the only sale for one day was a single, lonely geranium. She cried and felt like quitting, but with her honor at stake, and the determination of the samurai spirit, she persevered. She was the only employee for the first year, never taking a day off except for Thanksgiving and Christmas. The family farm laborer helped with cleaning, watering, and heavy lifting, but it was Mother who ran the nursery.

As the business continually grew year after year, Mother saved money. She made improvements to the property and looked for opportunities to meet the needs of her growing clientele. The property adjacent to the nursery became available. It was purchased as the business began to grow. The house became the new office, and she modified the pool to become a fishpond for Japanese koi or carp.

Even though Mother was not born with a green thumb, she was born with determination. She had the vision, guts, and the ability to see a silver lining in any situation. Mother raised six children and knew what it meant to persevere in good times and bad. She taught us to work hard, and she led by example: no one could work harder than Mother.

My mother was really telling me to go ahead and love life, to engage in it, give it all you've got. To love it with a passion.

—Dr. Maya Angelou

Today, Tsugawa Nursery occupies over seven acres, employs 40 people during the busy season, and is a destination nursery in the Pacific Northwest. Each year, loyal customers drive hundreds of miles in their trucks and vans to stock up on their favorite plants; a testament to the accomplishments of one woman's determination to never give up. My Mother understood the concept behind ganbaru: she knew that to succeed, whether in business or life, you have to expect both times of prosperity and times of want.

Mother knew the valleys only made the mountaintops that much sweeter. When asked about the success of Tsugawa Nursery, she replied,

> *Courage and family have kept me going.*
> *I have enjoyed the nursery, and I have come*
> *a long way from the dehydrated corn seeds!*
> *My advice to everyone is to believe that*
> *anything is possible and to never give up.*

I can still hear Mother's advice as I live my life. She always found a way to accomplish anything that was presented to her. She worked *circles* around everyone, and she also worked *miracles*. I sometimes think that she invented *multi-tasking!* Mother was an optimist, always believed in accomplishing the impossible, and never gave up. I miss her every day but her legacy continues.

> *The future belongs to those who believe*
> *in the beauty of their dreams.*

—Eleanor Roosevelt

In her later years, Mother enjoyed speaking with her loyal customers and finding the perfect plants for their yards and gardens. When summer arrived, she loved giving popsicles to young and old alike. It was a welcome treat, and it helped people to cool off.

After I finished writing the story of the nursery business, I read it to her. She commented, "Is that me...really?" Her health finally failed, and sadly, she passed away in 2011.

A true samurai, my mother, Mable Tsugawa, defines for me what ganbaru is all about. She never gave up, even after her only sale for the day was...one lonely geranium! What is the desire of your heart? What is your vision, dream, or goal? Is the desire strong enough that you will never give up until it is accomplished? Do you have what it takes? Can it be said of you, "He or she has ganbaru?"

The price of success is hard work,
dedication to the job at hand,
and the determination that whether we
win or lose, we have applied the
best of ourselves to the task at hand.

—Vince Lombardi

Final Note

The stories of individuals in this book include history, morals, ethics, business, personal development, and life. I have shared how the bushido code is a foundation or anchor that shaped character and lives. In writing this book, my message to you encompasses your life, thoughts, actions, deeds, and words. It is your uniqueness.

Now that you have read and absorbed the information, what actions will you take? I hope that you are inspired and empowered to apply the bushido code to your personal and business lives, like the samurai warriors of ancient Japan.

If a waterwheel exerts itself,
it has no time to get frozen.

—Japanese Proverb

Let's review what you have learned in this book.

- Courage
- Integrity
- Benevolence
- Respect
- Honesty
- Honor
- Loyalty
- Ganbaru

What goals, dreams, and visions do you have for your life? I believe you possess greatness and the ability to reach your desires. Your goals, dreams, and visions are in your heart for a reason and need to come to fruition; quite possibly they are your passionate purpose in life. Like the samurai, you can be the unstoppable force, achieving and fulfilling your purpose and highest leadership potential for the good of mankind. I challenge you to go for broke as you pursue your purpose in life!

The world is waiting for you to
unveil your gifts and talents.
What are you waiting for?

—Lori Tsugawa Whaley

I would love to hear from you, and I invite you to contact me at Lori@LoriWhaley.com. If this book has inspired and empowered you, your comments are welcome! It would be my honor to serve you on your journey through life coaching.

When applied to your business and life, the bushido code is a guiding light through the maze of life. Although you may not be facing the ultimate sacrifice, you are still engaged in a battle that requires strategy. Bushido is about doing the right thing all the time. In our modern society, I sense that we have lost our way. Our world is in dire need of true leaders. If ever there was a time for you to sharpen your sword and embrace your leadership role like the samurai ... that time is now!

I wish success and peace on your journey. All the best and God bless you!

When you link arms with this samurai woman,
you will never face your battle alone!

—Lori Tsugawa Whaley

Lori

Lori Tsugawa Whaley

About the Author

Lori Tsugawa Whaley is a third-generation Japanese American, and a descendant of the samurai. As a baby boomer, she grew up in a predominately Caucasian logging and farming community in rural southwest Washington. Lori's character and work ethic were formed by working hard alongside her parents on the family farm. She struggled with being different, especially during the school years.

As an adult, Lori channeled her energy into tireless research trying to understand her Japanese heritage. A lifelong desire led Lori and her husband on a trip to Japan. This first encounter with Japan fueled a yearning to dig deeper into her ancestral roots. She discovered that what she once scorned, she now warmly embraces.

Lori is on a mission to inspire individuals to apply the code of bushido (way of the warrior) to tap into their *soul* purpose in life. This will facilitate individuals and organizations to create their greatest leadership potential so they can live a powerful life of contribution far beyond their normal day-to-day existence.

The courage and compassion to guide others through tough times has been forged by her personal journey to regain wellness against demanding odds. Lori is a Traumatic Brain Injury (TBI) survivor.

Lori leads an active life, including volunteering for the YMCA for over 20 years. She is passionate about and enjoys Israeli folk dancing. Lori has been involved with Toastmasters for over 10 years, initially to overcome her fear of speaking. Professionally, Lori is a member of Association of Women Owned Business (AWOB).

Lori is proud and passionate about her Japanese heritage. She has traveled to Japan, speaks basic Japanese, and met her Tsugawa relatives during a trip to Japan. Lori is a member of the Japanese American Citizen League (JACL), U.S.-Japan Council (USJC), Japanese Cultural & Community Center of Washington (JCCCW), the Japan-America Society of the State of Washington (JASSW), and the Camp Harmony Committee. One of Lori's passions is to perform Japanese folk tales and dramas that involve using puppets for both young and old audiences.

A Pacific Northwest native, Lori graduated from Portland State University in 1978 with Honors. She has been married to husband John for nearly 40 years, and is the mother of two adult sons, a daughter-in-law, and is the doting grandmother of five adorable grandchildren, including identical twin girls! Lori and John reside in a Japanese-style country home in the Pacific Northwest.

PHOTOS

Masaichiro and Kazuno Tsugawa from Tokushima, Japan; the paternal grandparents of author. Photo courtesy of the Tsugawa family.

George and Mable Tsugawa, parents of author.
Photo courtesy of the Tsugawa Family.

Japanese diplomat, Chiune Sugihara.
Photo courtesy of John Whaley.

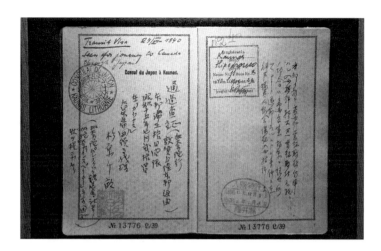

Sugihara visa at memorial museum in Yaotsu, Japan.

Photo courtesy of John Whaley.

Yaotsu, Gifu Prefecture, Japan. Hill of Humanity,
the memorial dedicated in honor of Chiune Sugihara.
Photo courtesy of Visas for Life Foundation.

Line at mess hall - Gila River War Relocation Center. Michi Nishiura Weglyn's residence during World War II. Photo courtesy of the War Relocation Center and Go For Broke National Education Center.

Life at Gila River War Relocation Center. Photo courtesy of the War Relocation Center and Go For Broke National Education Center.

The late Senator Daniel K. Inouye from Hawaii.

Dr. Toshio Inahara graduate of OHSU 1950. (Left)

Dr. Toshio Inahara graduate of University of Oregon Medical School, surgical practice. Photos courtesy of Dr. Toshio Inahara.

Uwajimaya - Flagship Store - Seattle, Washington.
Photo courtesy of John Whaley.

Moriguchi family at Uwajimaya.
Photo courtesy of the Moriguchi family.

Wakaji Matsumoto and family in front of photography studio located
in downtown Hiroshima two blocks from atomic bomb epicenter.
Photo courtesy of Hitoshi Ouchi and the City of Hiroshima Archives.

General Frank D. Merrill, Commanding General of the Merrill's
Marauders, presenting S/Sgt Roy Matsumoto the Legion of Merit for
his exploits at Walawbum, Burma on 5 March, 1944.
Photo courtesy of the Matsumoto family.

Roy Matsumoto in Washington, D.C., after receiving Congressional Gold Medal in 2010. Photo courtesy of the Matsumoto family.

Arthur Iwasaki saluting after receiving Congressional Gold Medal in 2010. Photo courtesy of the Iwasaki family.

George Tsugawa family - Brian and Lori (back) and
Mable and George Tsugawa (front) at Tsugawa Nursery in 2003.
Photo by L.E. Gaskow courtesy of *Portland Tribune*.

E Company, 2nd Battalion of the 442nd Regimental Combat Team
in formation. Camp Shelby, Mississippi. May 13, 1943. Courtesy of
the National Archives and Records Administration.

Nisei troops of Fourth Platoon, F Company, 2nd Battalion, 442nd
Regiment Combat Team, climb into a truck as they prepare to move
their bivouac area. Chambois Sector, France. October 14, 1944.
Courtesy of the National Archives and Records Administration.

Robert Shimada and Jinichi Miyashiro, members of the 100th
Infantry Battalion, set up a 60mm mortar. 1943. Courtesy of the
National Archives and Records Administration.

Members of the 522nd in action in the Bruyères Sector of France.
October 18, 1944. Courtesy of the United States Army Signal Corps.

MIS linguists "at work" in the office.
Courtesy of the National Archives and Records Administration and
Go For Broke National Education Center.

MIS linguists "at work" in the office.
Courtesy of the National Archives and Records Administration and
Go For Broke National Education Center.

The strain of 16 days of Battle For Leghorn shows in the faces of these Nisei soldiers of the 100th Infantry Battalion, as they leave on a regimental reserve U.S. Fifth Army. Castrellina Area, Italy. July 15, 1944.
Courtesy of the National Archives and Records Administration.

Nisei soldiers of the 2nd Battalion, 442nd Infantry Regiment, bow their heads in prayer for their departed comrades who gave their lives in combat with the enemy in the area north of Rome. The memorial services are being held at the Battalion headquarters area near Cecina. July 30, 1944.
Courtesy of the National Archives and Records Administration.

Samurai woman at the *Jidai Matsuri*, (Festival of the Ages), Kyoto, Japan 2012. Photo courtesy of John Whaley.

Samurai warriors at the Jidai Matsuri, Kyoto, Japan 2012. Photo courtesy of John Whaley.

Glossary

Bushido The honor code of the samurai that originated in feudal Japan. Deep roots in loyalty and obedience; it values honor above life itself.

Chuugi Loyalty - combination of two kanji; sincerity or loyalty, integrity, rectitude, justice, or correct action.

Daimyo A feudal lord who was a vassal of the shogun in Japan.

Domo arigato gozaimasu Thank you very much (polite).

Gaman To endure the unbearable with patience, dignity, and self-control. A virtue or trait to do your best during distressful times.

Ganbaru To tenaciously continue through tough times. Don't give up, try your hardest, and go for broke are expressions associated with ganbaru.

Gi Integrity - justice and moral righteousness.

Haiku Japanese poetry with 17 syllables.

Issei A first-generation Japanese immigrant to the United States.

Jin Benevolence - disposition to do good, an act of kindness, and a generous gift.

Kamon Refers specifically to emblems used to identify a family; a crest.

Kanji A system of Japanese writing mainly derived from Chinese characters/ideograms.

Katabami Wood sorrel leaves that are portrayed with sword blades on warrior class kamon.

Ken A sword; a sabre.

Kibei A person of Japanese descent who was born in the United States but later lived and was educated in Japan.

Koshogumi Part of the elite guard forces, a position of rank from which most magistracies were chosen.

Makoto Honesty - combination of two kanji; to speak and to accomplish.

Meishi A Japanese business card.

Meiyo Honor - to have an admired or praiseworthy reputation.

Mon An encompassing term that refers to the Japanese emblems used to identify an individual or family.

Ninja A member of a feudal Japanese society of mercenary agents. They were highly trained in martial arts and hired for covert purposes, i.e., espionage, sabotage, and assassination.

Nisei A person of Japanese descent (second generation) who was born and educated in the United States or Canada.

Obaasan A term of respect given to female elders meaning grandmother.

Ojiisan A term of respect given to male elders meaning grandfather.

Rei Respect - rite or ceremony, morality, and politeness.

Ronin A samurai who is masterless and no longer serving a daimyo, or feudal lord.

Samurai   A member of the warrior class in
                   Japan from 1185-1867. Samurai
                   literally means "one who serves."
                   They lived by the bushido code and
                   were willing to give their lives to
                   defend their honor.

Sansei   A person of Japanese descent (third
                   generation), grandchild of Japanese
                   immigrants to the United States or
                   Canada.

Sensei   A teacher, master or instructor; a title
                   of respect.

Shigakko   Private centers for the instruction of
                   samurai youth, also known as warrior
                   schools or samurai schools.

Shogun   Literally means general or military
                   commander. After the end of the
                   12th century, the shogun was the
                   hereditary official governing Japan.

Wa   Usually translated into English as
                   peace and/or harmony; a Japanese
                   cultural concept.

Yen   Japanese basic monetary unit.

Yuuki   Courage - kanji combining the action
                   of heroism with the concept of spirit of
                   mind resulting in bravery of spirit.

終わり